T0146600

The Sanctuary of My Solitude

The Sanctuary of My Solitude

The Thoughts, Feelings, and Life Lessons of an Imperfect Christian

Anthony Giesick

iUniverse®

THE SANCTUARY OF MY SOLITUDE
THE THOUGHTS, FEELINGS, AND LIFE LESSONS
OF AN IMPERFECT CHRISTIAN

iUniverse books may be ordered through booksellers or by contacting:

iUniverse
1663 Liberty Drive
Bloomington, IN 47403
www.iuniverse.com
1-800-Authors (1-800-288-4677)

ISBN: 978-1-5320-3601-9 (sc)
ISBN: 978-1-5320-3602-6 (e)

Library of Congress Control Number: 2017918066

Print information available on the last page.

iUniverse rev. date: 01/17/2018

Table of Contents

An introduction:

My name is Anthony Giesick. I was born in California in 1987. When I was a young child, my parents separated. Due to the fact that my parents were separated, I was raised by my mother, grandmother and my older brother and sister. I was born with Cerebral Palsy, which affected the left side of my body, which kept me from fully participating in more sports games or physical activity. Also, I wasn't too interested in most sports. I often separated myself from my fellow peers, often making me feel like an outcast among my peers. Due to this outcast, I struggled with shyness and making friends. I often found myself stuck in my own head, thinking through deep thoughts and unconventional ideas. As I developed into a young boy, I realized that I loved stories and creative ideas.

At the age of ten I moved in with my father to Phoenix, Arizona. I had to learn to meet new people and make friends all over again. Yes, that was a struggle, but I always seemed to find a small group of friends over the years. I was never extremely popular, but I was not unpopular simply, resting nicely in between.

Early in my years I began writing! My creative mind formed stories, poems, songs and many things in between. I had a lot to say, and I had many ways that could be used to say it.

Hip Hop:

Throughout my life I've loved Hip Hop. I love the poetry of forming words to create a story. I love the way that poetry, through Hip Hop, was used to express the thoughts, feelings and emotions of the artist who wrote the words. Soon, I found myself attaching my attentions to the skillful art of these modern day poets. I quickly bought the albums of my favorite artists, quickly ripping open the packaging and listening to the record continuously, memorizing every lyric. Through the elements of Hip Hop generation after generation are able to connect with the artist as well as the audience. As we listen to the poems that the artist is performing, there is a connection that breaks barriers and brings together humans from various backgrounds and cultures.

I Love Hip Hop!

Before I knew it, I was creating sentences that rhymed and telling stories that eventually declared every aspect of my life. It started out as a hobby, a way of having fun with this amazing art form and it quickly became my talent. A talent that would teach me about life, allow me to deal with the various trials that I will eventually face as well as teach me about myself. I could always depend on my writing to complete me. Over the years I kept writing, feeling like I was developing something that would one day impact the world around me. I was writing something that would connect the hearts of those who read it.

The Sanctuary of my Solitude

The following collection of this book, "The Sanctuary of my Solitude" is the first collection of poems. This collection of poems/songs was written between 2010 and 2012. At the time that these poems were written, I was in college and living in Flagstaff, Arizona. At this point in my life I was in my first real romantic relationship and I had realizations of myself in the context of a relationship as well as my behaviors in my solitude. Throughout this following collection of poems, I walk you through many of these realizations; such as, my ability to hide my true feelings within the context of my poems, my realization that my behaviors also have destructive consequence for myself. Through this collection of poems, you are walked through my relationship with God and the guidance that I received from my Heavenly Father.

I was given the privilege of writing about the darkness that rested within my heart and mind. The purpose of sharing my darkness was simply to help relate to people who read through the poems. I was able to share my conversations with God when it comes to my romantic relationships. I was also able to speak on the "mask" that I wear in this world that I live in; a world where your public persona may be different than the mask that is revealed in private. I was able to express the first steps that I was forced to take when trusting Jesus with my life while finishing college and trying to begin a career in teaching.

"The Sanctuary of my Solitude" is a journey of a growing boy, moving from adolescence to young adulthood while, at the same time, trusting Jesus throughout the process. This collection delves into the deepest parts of my thoughts during this time, while at the same time documenting my growth and development throughout the process.

My Mask

My day goes by and I finally see,
Just who I am and the image I see.
Now I wonder who I am supposed to be.
Maybe one day I will be set free.
But I continue to wear my mask,
Waiting for the day when my past is passed.
Hoping to see the new life I've asked
To develop, hoping it lasts.
Now, I look in the mirror, deep in my eyes,
I feel my pain, and I feel my lies.
I wear my mask as my disguise;
Never truly knowing the "how's" or the "whys."
So, what can I do to change my past?
What can I do to walk with God on my new path?
I won't have to worry if I won't last,
And I will never be forced to wear this mask.

I put on this mask,
I wonder what becomes of me.
Is this my face?
Is all this the sum of me?
My heart won't last,
Someone new has come from me.
Is this my new place?
I think I have come for me.
I take off this mask,
Showing what only some will see.
This is my face,
What will become of me?
I know that I won't last,
Even I try to run from me.
But I can't win the chase,
My true self shows up eventually.

Every day I wake up and try to be,
The exact opposite of what I am, but I can't lie to me.
You see, I see who I am, the dark side of me.
Apparently, it was only me who was the only who lied to me.
Like claiming to be the brother that I knew I wasn't.
I wasn't showing love with all of the hitting and all of the shoving.
The anger of my past bruised your bodies for nothing,
I can't believe I did this to prove that I'm something.
See, you thought I loved you, but of course I did,
But I couldn't get passed what my past has hid.
I just re-lived the pain I never felt as a kid.
This is no way let your little brother live.
As I speak these words, I hope they pass
Because the bond we have is sure to last.
But the fear inside just adds new math
Because every day I wake up, I must put on the mask.

I put on this mask,
I wonder what becomes of me.
Is this my face?
Is all this the sum of me?
My heart won't last,
Someone new has come from me.
Is this my new place?
I think I have come for me.
I take off this mask,
Showing what only some will see.
This is my face,
What will become of me?
I know that I won't last,
Even I try to run from me.
But I can't win the chase,
My true self shows up eventually.

I look into the mirror; I see exactly who I am.
Knowing that I can't show me, I place the mask in my hand,

Pull it over my face and smile for all I can,
Never revealing the monster inside of this man;
I just continue to cover my identity.
I hide my ugliness from the world, I'm an entity,
Maybe I am not supposed to show who I am, it's not meant to be.
Maybe that's why I dig through the truth, to see what it meant to me.
The monster inside runs and courses through my veins;
It destroys who I want to be until only guilt remains.
Then the guilt built up until that was my frame,
And I can't get out of this box, it becomes my name.
How can I break this box and express myself?
Allowing people to see how I see myself,
Because I can't reveal my face to say that I need your help,
My mask has become a part of me, those are just the card I'm dealt.

I put on this mask,
I wonder what becomes of me.
Is this my face?
Is all this the sum of me?
My heart won't last,
Someone new has come from me.
Is this my new place?
I think I have come for me.
I take off this mask,
Showing what only some will see.
This is my face,
What will become of me?
I know that I won't last,
Even I try to run from me.
But I can't win the chase,
My true self shows up eventually.

Path of Destruction

It seems that I don't even know who I am,
I look into the mirror and don't recognize the man that stands.
His face looks like mine, but the image I don't understand.
I don't know what to do; I don't know where to land.
How could I act this way after all I was taught?
Looking back on all the evil actions that I sought,
Never knowing, never showing exactly what I am not.
I continue to walk in the same path the enemy plots.
Daily it talks to me, in my ears it echoes,
Never knowing what to hear, the words stack like Legos
Never to fall, but I couldn't do anything but let go.
And in that I listen as he waves and says, "Let's go."
My life gets darker in a night, as I am shattered,
I follow, I'm Hollow, and it seems that nothing else mattered.
I begin to feel like myself, I am able to see the pattern,
I've felt that way before, climbing the depression ladder.

This has all happened before,
I've walked down this path of destruction.
It seems I can't close the door,
It's then that my mind suffers from corruption.
My pain grows sore,
Soon I feel like nothing.
This has happened before.
This has all happened before,
I've walked down this path of destruction.
It seems I can't close the door,
It's then that my mind suffers from corruption.
My pain grows sore,
Soon I feel like nothing.
This has happened before.

As night comes, I lay and toss and turn in my bed,
I hear what is said and repeatedly punch myself in the head.
I don't want to solve my problems; I want to do this instead,
Because I can't be happy, I need that level of continuous dread.
I clinch my fist as my fears begin feeding his calls,
I'm believing this all, as it stings, I swing at the walls.
I know I will fall, but I try to fight as my skin starts to crawl.
Is this all? I've lived this way, not knowing what to do at all.
The words take over me, it's like the action's not mine.
I become blind, unsure what will happen next in this line.
There is a sign that shows exactly how I'm falling behind.
My fight's declined; the infection now grows into my mind.
I start to feel like I'm worthless; my abuse grows an extension,
I cause all of this pain on purpose, hoping to get some attention.
But I turn down all help whenever any attention is mentioned;
I know that real help will cause me to leave this depressing dimension.

This has all happened before,
I've walked down this path of destruction.
It seems I can't close the door,
It's then that my mind suffers from corruption.
My pain grows sore,
Soon I feel like nothing.
This has happened before.
This has all happened before,
I've walked down this path of destruction.
It seems I can't close the door,
It's then that my mind suffers from corruption.
My pain grows sore,
Soon I feel like nothing.
This has happened before.

We're back together, picking right where we left off,
Nothing has changed; it seems that all I can do is step off.
I do what he wants, knowing he will guide me, let's set off.
I am ready to go, this realm likes me, now let's talk.

See realistically my misery shows through on my face,
So instantly, I feel differently, I do believe I 'm awake.
And then I see the recipe bubble over and trace;
It creates exactly who I am as I continue hating this place.
And I begin swinging and punching, just trying to cause harm.
I'm hoping that when you see it, there will be no cause for alarm.
But I know that there is as I look at the bruise in my arm
And above my eye, but I am not ready for charm.
I can't be healed; my misery makes me feel human.
It all makes me feel normal, yet, it makes me feel ruined.
It just makes me feel abandoned; Is this what I'm pursuing?
I guess I won't know, so just listen and see everything that I'm doing.

This has all happened before,
I've walked down this path of destruction.
It seems I can't close the door,
It's then that my mind suffers from corruption.
My pain grows sore,
Soon I feel like nothing.
This has happened before.
This has all happened before,
I've walked down this path of destruction.
It seems I can't close the door,
It's then that my mind suffers from corruption.
My pain grows sore,
Soon I feel like nothing.
This has happened before.

Let You Down

I sit in this room, all alone with the silence.
I listen to my thoughts, which beats me into silence.
With every moment that passed, I just can't seem to move.
I seem stuck in this rut; I just don't know what to do.
I can feel your frustration in every text that you sent.
I felt every word burn; it seems it just wouldn't relent.
It seems that the truth is revealed about the truth I've been hiding,
I hide the truth from my family to keep the truth from igniting.
I don't how to fight; it just seems that I've lost.
I am unsure who I am, so I can't see the cost.
So, I pick my pen again, just hoping to cope,
but the written word is as important as the ones that are spoke.
So, if I can't speak it, what's the point to this language?
It's the fact that I don't speak that I've caused all this anguish.
How can I tell the truth when all I'm hearing are lies?
I hear the same lies that cause me to buckle and cry.

I let you down. Now, I sit here quiet and trapped.
I let you down. I am unsure who we are.
I let you down. I will never know how to act.
I let you down. I never thought we'd be so far apart.

Now that I think of you, this question runs through my mind,
how can I love you when it seems that I don't have a spine?
I just fall to the floor, my body begins to quiver and shake,
and it seems I can't wait, but I am collapsing because the pain is too great.
I want to tell the world, I want to scream it from the roof tops,
but every time the subject comes up, I get queasy then I can't talk.
With everyday that goes by, you get more and more hurt.
I wish I could take your pain, but I can't, so this won't work.
How could our relationship last if I can't be honest?
I feel weak, apparently I don't know what strong is.

I feel I am falling apart from the inside out,
I can't cry out because then the truth will fly out.
My heart beats fast, my stomach is tied in a knot,
and I can't even imagine what you might have thought.
You must think I'm a loser, just a waste of your time,
I'm waiting to find what will happen, please give me a sign.

I let you down. Now, I sit here quite and trapped.
I let you down. I am unsure who we are.
I let you down. I will never know how to act.
I let you down. I never thought we'd be so far apart.

You are all I have; I just hope that you see
how special you are, even though I am not free.
It looks as if I can't be the man I know you deserve;
just knowing that I fall short has my body un-nerved.
I know I can change, I just had to take the first step,
But I've lost all will, I guess this something I have to except.
The answer's in my head, just won't listen to reason.
I listen to demons in my head, cause my screaming.
The lies that they tell seem so vivid and real,
there's no deal, the truth I have is now theirs to steal.
But the only one that's hurt seems to be you in this process.
Let's be honest, I'm too scared to fulfill my first promise.
So, for that I am truly sorry and all I can say
is I hope you find happiness to please you one day.
and as the time goes by, I'll just sit here waiting,
hoping I'll still be around when you find true love isn't fading.

I let you down. Now, I sit here quite and trapped.
I let you down. I am unsure who we are.
I let you down. I will never know how to act.
I let you down. I never thought we'd be so far apart.

I Can Hear His voice (part one)

KD: "The night grew cold and still as I lay there.
The night grew, I couldn't feel, I had to stay there.
My heart fell as if I knew what it would stay there.
The words sunk in, I knew my mind wouldn't play fair."
Devil's voice (DV): "Hi, do you remember me? It's me, your conscience,
and I am here to settle your mind from the jumble of your conflicts.
First off, I want to tell you, you're not ready.
You may think you are, but the burden you bear will be heavy."
KD: "What do you mean 'be heavy'? I don't understand it.
Isn't this supposed to happen? Tell me, I can't stand it."
DV: "You think you are ready to be a husband and then a father?
Look at your own father and don't bother.
I know you think it will be different, but it won't be.
You will stumble in his footsteps, and that you can quote me.
You will end up just like him, don't lie to yourself."
KD: "I'm not! I know I can do it! I didn't ask for your help!"

I can hear his voice
as it echoes through my ears.
The words he speaks
initiates my fears.
I can hear his voice
is what He said true?
I don't know what will happen;
I don't know what to do...
when I hear His voice.

DV: "First off, stop there and let me ask you a question,
how are you ready when you are so scared of the progression?
Let's just take a look at your life and then we'll decide,
you are pushing 22 and still too scared to learn to drive.
What are you going to do with a family? How will you function?

Are you just going to hope everything turn out alright and wait for destruction?"

KD: "No, I am going to learn, I still have time,"

DV: "but time's is running short, you have to have an idea in mind.
Anyway, let me ask; what are you going to do for a job now?
You have never worked; don't you see that as rather odd now?"

KD: "Leave me alone! Stop it! You have no idea what you speak of,
My God has a plan for me, only through Him will I reach love."

DV: "Ok, stop right there, let's just take time to look back a second,
Did God say that He had a plan for you? Do you really feel directed?
See, I am always here for you, no matter what you what you go through.
You are me, I am you. So, how well do you think I know you?"

I can hear his voice
as it echoes through my ears.
The words he speaks
initiates my fears.
I can hear his voice
is what He said true?
I don't know what will happen;
I don't know what to do...
when I hear His voice.

KD: "Do I believe in what I am hearing? Is this the voice of my life?
If what he says is true, than how can I truly follow my Christ?
I tried to find something better; maybe I was in the wrong?
Now, I don't know when to go, maybe I was right all along?"

DV: "Yes, listen to me because there is something I have to bring up.
Your girl doesn't really love you; I think it's time to break up."

KD: "No, I know that she loves me, she tells me every day."

DV: "Okay, stop right there and just listen to what I say,
she expresses her love with words, but how often does she show it?
Real love is expressed physically; I know you already know it.
Now, let's look at when you are together, the affection you initiate it.
And remember when you try to get close, she stops, it's like she truly hates it."

KD: "Okay, I have to stop there, I can't listen any further, and this can't be true because I know you are just trying to hurt her."

DV: "No, I am not trying to hurt her, I am just giving you the truth, and I just hope that you can find the truth, looking at your whole life for proof."

KD: "I can't believe this, are you sure this is all true?"

DV: "Every word of it."

KD: "I can't...I can't believe it. It can't be true. I can't....I can't listen to this anymore."

DV: "It's true, all of it."

KD: "No, it can't be. God is true, isn't he? God will provide, Won't He? I mean, He can guide me. He will guide me."

DV: "Do you really believe that?"

KD: "I do! I do!"

DV: "Where is your God now?"

I Can Hear His voice (Part two)

KD: "Father, I really need you. I need some direction in my life. I am being told these lies. I don't know what if they are real. I don't know what to believe. I need you."

KD: "I don't know what to do as the sweat beads off my chest.
I hear every word he spoke; it seems I will never get rest.
I know what I hear are lies, but the truth is not far behind.
Oh, God! How did this happen? Please get this demon out of my mind."
Devil's voice (DV): "Look I am no demon, but part of you, why can't you get that?"
KD: "Stop it! I denounce you; Get out of here, Get back!"
I don't believe in what you speak, I don't believe in what I hear."
DV: "Why? I don't speak anything that you don't already fear."
KD: "The words sunk in, I felt the lump in my throat,
and my chest grew tight with the new word I never spoke.
I couldn't believe the words I heard, although my mind said they were true.
God, I can't bare this anymore, please help, I need you."
God's voice (GV): "Son, I am here for you, please know that I hear your cries,
I ask that you leave, imposter, we don't need to hear your lies.
All you speak is wickedness, and you prey on the weak,
but I demand you leave this man, he is mine to keep."

I can hear his voice
as it echoes through my ears.
The word HE speaks
illuminates my fears.
I can hear his voice
I know what He says is true
I don't know what will happen,
but I do know what to do...
when I hear His voice.

KD: "God is that you? I knew that you would come for me."
GV: "How dare you! You have no power to speak on what my son will be.
His life is in my hands, only I know what his future holds,
and trust me, I will be guiding him as the story of his life unfolds."
DV: "Are you kidding me? Do you really believe these tales?
I mean they are rediculess, there's no way you can break these spells."
GV: "He can and he will! I have spoken it and so it is!"
KD: "Thank you Father, I am forever grateful for what you did.
God, hear my voice. I know that what he said was false.
I believe your promises, and I want to give you all my faults.
I want to give you all my life, I just want to follow you,
But I hear these lies and I follow in their hallow views."
DV: "These words aren't lies, these words are his thoughts and feelings,
He fears these words, and it's just his own future he fears he's killing."
GV: "Bite your tongue! Don't talk just to speak your language!
I am the I AM; only I can heal this boy's anguish."

I can hear his voice
as it echoes through my ears.
The word HE speaks
illuminates my fears.
I can hear his voice
I know what He says is true
I don't know what will happen,
but I do know what to do...
when I hear His voice.

KD: "I began to rest, my heart was filled with the words He spoke,
I know my future, and my life is strong and filled with hope.
I want to follow in your plan, God! I want to see just what you have!
I want to know you with all my being! I want to walk down your path."
GV: "Well, my son, I have a plan for you. You have a path to take,
your life is forever in my hands, and your life was never a mistake."
KD: "Thank you for carrying me, I am sorry I don't always see it.
I see your influence! You opened my mind, my heart you freed it."
GV: "You are welcome, my child and trust I will never leave,

I will always be here to guide you, and I just ask that you follow me."
KD: "But what do I do when the lies arise again?
The words burn me; I ask when will it end?"
GV: "I am sorry to say it doesn't, the tempting will remain;
but remember that I am here and nothing can stop my reign."
KD: "Thank you, Father! I see your love for is new,
I can hear your voice and I know that what you say is true."

I can hear his voice
as it echoes through my ears.
The word HE speaks
illuminates my fears.
I can hear his voice
I know what He says is true
I don't know what will happen,
but I do know what to do...
when I hear His voice.

I Know Today

If I let the Devil talk to me, whispering to me at night,
his "truth" will soak into me and truthfully I just might
loose fights, giving me the truth of new sights.
I can't choose right because truthfully I know that I'd lose sight
of what God's got for me and what he has given,
because now I'm driven on the world that He is living.
But I can't say living, I'm wondering what to do,
which means there's one thing that I could really do
and that one thing is forever listen to you.
One thing is true; I know I can make it through.
Because His word gives me the power that I can pull through
and I don't have to live my life constantly in déjà vu.
I can be renewed; I am given a new path.
New dashes that show who I am, yeah, let's do that.
You see, I knew that my life is His, a true fact.
So, I just give my fight to Him and I move back.

I know today is a new day, dreaming.
I know today is a new day now.
I know today I must face my demons.
I know today that I won't back down.
Because everyday it's your face I'm seeing.
Because everyday it'd to you I bow.
Because everyday it's for truth I'm freeing.
Because you're the one who wears the crown now.

You see, I'm coming back with a vengeance; I pick up the pen to strike.
And you can easily listen to the words and think you know what it's like.
But the ink soaks in, as I bleed through the paper tonight,
and I share my heart with you while you ignore what I write.
But you see, he doesn't; so it seems that the Devil will invite,
my thoughts in him, and then corrupt them, just trying to change my
insight.

Now the time has come, now I know that he is finished.
I know I can't run, but I know his sting has diminished.
It no longer hurts; everything that he says is pure gimmicks.
God's word reigns, He shows me how I need to live it.
I know it's time to face my demons, go after them with the mouth of God!
The Devil's doubts are gone; it looks like he's out of a job!
I am standing strong, so I will never turn away.
I turn to God, I learn of God; now all I can do is learn to pray.
I'll run it back, with the LORD I'll stomp the Devil right in his tracks,
and lay him flat, and still have strength at t he end of that.

I know today is a new day, dreaming.
I know today is a new day now.
I know today I must face my demons.
I know today that I won't back down.
Because everyday it's your face I'm seeing.
Because everyday it's to you I bow.
Because everyday it's for truth I'm freeing.
You're the one who wears the crown now.

I'm ready to take the mic back, press it to my lips and speak my peace.
I will not feast on my emotions; I don't ever need to feed that beast.
I will just continue to turn to God's and be released.
I am unleashed; I can at least say that to say the least.
What else can I say? The past is gone, so why dwell on it?
I've seen the past hung up, it's no longer an issue I can't prevail on it.
So, I give my past to Him, He gave me life, give it back to Him.
I throw it all into His hands; I guess you can say it was passed to Him.
So, the Devil can try to speak to me, whisper into my eardrum,
telling me lustful lies, but with God being louder, I will never hear them.
So, I will continue to battle, fight for my freedom at hand.
I'm free in this land, but trapped in my head, I need to expand.
It's time to jump out on faith, just to see where I can land.
Cause only by doing that can I learn who I am.
And I am not finished, I know I can only do what I can,

that's why I thank God that I can say this as I stand.
I know today is a new day, dreaming.
I know today is a new day now.
I know today I must face my demons.
I know today that I won't back down.
Because everyday it's your face I'm seeing.
Because everyday it's to you I bow.
Because everyday it's for truth I'm freeing.
You're the one who wears the crown now.

Let the Grenade Drop

Look into my eyes, no lies; you'll see the truth that relies within.
I will never cry again, I can only get up and try again.
I will tell the truth, the entire truth,
I will never purposely mislead the youth.
I will guide them as if they were my troops.
It's time to stand firm, so lace up your boots.
So, let the words you say mean what they say,
I will never say something I don't mean, so let's say
Every word that is said has a purpose and meaning to it.
I will stand on what I said; it's finally time to do it.
There have been too many times that my mind would hold back,
I would never speak, when I should have told that.
But the time has come for my mind to run,
My mouth was to speak the truth where the light was shunned.
Now, I lunge toward the ones who beat me down, I can't run.
It's just begun, the battle's won, it's time to put them on the run, and
I'm done.

Let the grenade drop,
Let the place blow.
Let the world shake,
You're letting your faith show.
Let your views build,
Let your thoughts flow.
It's time to bring a change,
So let your past go.

I know you think you know me, but I believe you are confused,
I've got new views to express, so let's light up the fuse.
But I will never be hurt by the ones who refuse
To get to know me, I am no longer singing the blues.
I will just continue to do what I do,
I'm breaking through to you all because I am feeling brand new.

And you really want me to write that too?
Fine, it's time to come through just to see what you might do.
But this is it; I will not be taken down from where I stand,
I am the man who devised a plan.
You can't tell me I can't because I know I can.
Now, all I have to do is to get you to understand.
See, I will always be the person that I say I am.
Why lie to you when the spoken truth has a harder hand?
Why cry to you when the tear's dry when it lands?
And I am already at a point where I know where to stand.

Let the grenade drop,
Let the place blow.
Let the world shake,
You're letting your faith show.
Let your views build,
Let your thoughts flow.
It's time to bring a change,
So let your past go.

I know you want me to write a rhyme just to get your respect.
Don't forget, I'm my own person, my own prospect.
I don't listen to you, so don't try to project
Your negativity on my words and the thoughts I protect.
Look into my eyes, you can see the determination.
Word formation used to break down expectations.
So, there's no faking in the rhymes that I'm making,
Only true breaking and there are more lines for the taking.
So, let the rhyme build up, just listen to the delivery.
A perfect romance, there no death in this Chivalry.
So, follow the words, let the rhymes speak for them self.
All in due time, the lines won't keep to itself.
So, let's say these words, let's live for the cause,
Not wrapped in a pause, let the words create applause
It's in your heart and your soul inside.
Let's not hide, why not learn from the tears we've cried?

Let the grenade drop,
Let the place blow.
Let the world shake,
You're letting your faith show.
Let your views build,
Let your thoughts flow.
It's time to bring a change,
So let your past go.

No apologies

I'm sitting here looking at the blank page and I get depressed,
Knowing that I should write words for this age, but I'm not impressed.
Every word that I put up on this page I could never flex,
But I will never fall under the weight. Well, I guess then that the test,
Because every word I write is for one, so I will give nothing less,
Than my best, just my breath, I'm not looking for anything less than His perfectness.
So you look at me, what do you see?
Do you see a man who strives to live his life so perfectly?
He see hurt and he works to see,
If he can alleviate the pain, he's working. He
Turns to God, He allows the words to guide as they soak in.
Applying the words to his life, He doesn't apologies for how the word coats him.
He only keeps going, keeps growing, showing who he is as the LORD coaxed him,
He's allowing him to show love to the exact same world that broke him.
He has a new life, new heights tonight; I might fight for the sight He has given me.
Tonight might be the night that I give you insight of Christ because how He lives in me.
He is living see, He has given me a new attitude and I will not apologize for his gift for me.

No matter what has happened,
No matter what I face.
I will stand firm in your love.
I will stand firm in your grace.
So, expect no sympathy from me
This is how I am supposed to be.
Never expect a sorry from me,
There are no apologies for God's grace.

Just so you know, there will never be a time where I will be counted out,
I can count it now because there will be a time where your amount is out.
The doubt will sprout, but my God stands firm and the crowd will shout,
His name, His fame, can you see the amount that He counts?
The clock will tick, so just watch your watch as the seconds go,
And maybe you can see why I set to be free while you write your reckless flow,
I'm waiting for the time to blow while your audience forgets your infectious flow.
The best will go to a new place where we will be able to see His second show.
So, why would I ever let you come up and talk me out of this?
No doubt in this will grow as long as I seek God and learn to walk out in bliss.
The route is this, walk in Faith and He will build you up so you can walk out in this.
So, why would I ever turn my back on His grace just to learn your doubts amiss?
So, the time has come for us to change and live by our conviction,
A new transition as I grow in to the life of a new creation, a new Christian.
As I grow and transform, I will live by a new story and a new vision,
So, try to tell me this isn't right as you see the life that I am now living.

No matter what has happened,
No matter what I face.
I will stand firm in your love.
I will stand firm in your grace.
So, expect no sympathy from me
This is how I am supposed to be.
Never expect a sorry from me,
There are no apologies for God's grace.

No matter what happens I will never forget,
Who you made me out to be, no matter the threats,
Because you made me out for me, it's time to go, get set,
Let's run the race at an unsafe pace to see the face of the elect.

I made a promise and I will not let that fall through.
Regardless of how you look at me because I know it's all true.
"The truth will set you free." How could you know that if it's something you won't do?
I walk in the truth of God while you live in a view a skewed.
So, you can mock me for my walking, you could never understand it,
Trying to demand it, but you never listen the truth is handed.
No, you would rather build your views than truly expand it.
But I will not follow you in your hurt when the truth's so easily planted.
Now, you can look to the LORD's word, or you could choose to ignore it.
But never look down at me for my strength to choose to live for it.
But even if you do look at me oddly I will continue to adore it,
Because His was spent and I know my life could never afford it. so.....

No matter what has happened,
No matter what I face.
I will stand firm in your love.
I will stand firm in your grace.
So, expect no sympathy from me
This is how I am supposed to be.
Never expect a sorry from me,
There are no apologies for God's grace.

You love me

I am still here, even though I'm broken hearted,
I am on my knees, and I guess this is where the story started.
LORD, I need you; this is all that I will ever know.
LORD, I want you; I am tired of saying no.
I disgrace you Father and you still give love.
You gave love, giving up your life and your blood.
What can I do? LORD, what can I say?
I don't deserve this, but you gave to me anyway.
I walk away from you! Why did you choose me?
Would your Glory be different if you lose me?
NO! You'll still be God, the Creator and the Lamb;
you will still be Glorious, even if I don't understand.
So, why did you save me, pulling me from my sinful nature?
Why did you pull me out, allowing me to meet my maker?
I guess I may never know, I may never get it,
but I know you are True, I can never forget it.

You love me, I guess I won't understand.
I shrug you, trying to be my own man.
I walk from you and I still can't believe,
that you tell me that you won't leave.
You stand there, you show me you give grace,
I walk to you; I just want to see your face.

Now, I ask why you saved, but you made me to love,
but I couldn't love because I didn't have the love of your hug.
Now, all I can do is take your love and except it,
that means I show you love, I was never rejected.
Now, I am on my knees, please hear my pleas,
I need to realize your grace, I need to know why you bleed.
I let the blood wash over me; I let you know it all.
I want to cry into your arms, in your presents I will fall.
Father, just let me grow, let me walk in your steps;

let me follow you, but I need to read your text.
I still have questions in my mind, all I can do is ask,
and give you my future because you already fixed my past.
You took my pain and allowed me to become new,
I'm a new creature with a new mind, and you helped me get through.
Now, I'm in your heart and your word is deep in mine,
and I know you are true, glorious and perfectly divine.

You love me, I guess I won't understand.
I shrug you, trying to be my own man.
I walk from you and I still can't believe,
that you tell me that you won't leave.
You stand there, you show me you give grace,
I walk to you; I just want to see your face.

Now, I sit here thinking of all that you did,
the life that you lived and gave so that I could live.
You gave the lashes, the beating, the scars, and the crown,
you gave the blood that you spilled and left on the ground.
I couldn't believe you do that! You allowed that to happen.
Now, I learn to rest in you, I get to see your compassion.
A compassion that builds me into something different,
a difference that allows me to follow you in an insistent.
Now, I see you all, and I want to give you more.
I want you to have everything, God's love galore.
You see, you gave everything so that I can be with you,
and all I can do is give you all, because I know you are true.
Your word is illuminated for me as I read,
beginning to learn of you and how you set me free.
I will never believe what you did to make me stand,
and just for me to know you and to know you made me who I am.

You love me, I guess I won't understand.
I shrug you, trying to be my own man.
I walk from you and I still can't believe,
that you tell me that you won't leave.
You stand there, you show me you give grace,
I walk to you; I just want to see your face.

Let it Shine

"Let your light so shine before men, that they may see your good works, and glorify your Father which is in heaven." Matthew 5:16

A select few, chosen: my new light, glowing.
A heart of a man after God: new life showing.
I no longer live fiercely.
I'm just hoping to know my God, do you all hear me?
I never can stop; I'm a light on a hill.
Just living my days, know God has me filled.
Now, my life has direction, destination I'm heading.
My destiny's been set, thank God for my setting.
I walk in my grace, I acknowledge His attributes.
Perfect in holiness, under God's control I don't have to choose.
So, I walk in my calling, place my feet in the sand prints.
A life with God, great! I pray you all will understand this.
Can I go back? Never! Why would I ever choose to?
God and I together, no longer live the way fools do.
I just keep on living; let my life be the light.
The world will see because God's glory is bright.

A light now lives in you.
Let it shine! Let it shine!
A new spirit has been given you.
Let it shine! Let it shine!
Your life's chosen for this path.
Let it shine! Let it shine!
His grace has freed you from wrath.
Let it shine! Let it shine!
If you've got a light in your heart!
Let it shine! Let it shine!
If you're living a new start!
Let it shine! Let it shine!
If by His grace you've been saved!

Let it shine! Let it shine!
Since you're no longer in a grave!
Let it shine! Let it shine!

Awake! Awake! Put on strength!
Darkness sinks in; turn your light on, great!
Let your world see your love, please don't wait.
Let your life grow; watch it lift up the weight.
Allow change to take hold as you grow in faith.
Let it grow and shape as you show your place.
While the world may attack you at a moment or instance,
Your strength in persistence will show because of your difference.
So, no matter what you face, face it with Bible in hand.
Survival's the plan, so why not live a life with a righteous stand?
I'm tired of letting this life take me down, I can't breathe.
But now I serve a God who wears the crown, death leave!
No grave for me, His grace lets me live.
Put the brave in me as I live to give.
A new life in love: a new day in light.
A new sight to see: a way away from night.

A light now lives in you.
Let it shine! Let it shine!
A new spirit has been given you.
Let it shine! Let it shine!
Your life's chosen for this path.
Let it shine! Let it shine!
His grace has freed you from wrath.
Let it shine! Let it shine!
If you've got a light in your heart!
Let it shine! Let it shine!
If you're living a new start!
Let it shine! Let it shine!
If by His grace you've been saved!
Let it shine! Let it shine!
Since you're no longer in a grave!
Let it shine! Let it shine!

God is Great!

"God is great!" I've heard that before.
But without him, what am I rapping for?
Because every word I write, whether light or dark,
They have His fingerprint, it has His mark.
Day-to-day, Night-to-night:
I fight for the light, even when it shows I have no might
.

What can I say? His hand is on my shoulder, guiding me.
Because of him I've seen the world, he's not hiding me.
So, stand up for your beliefs, live life to the fullest.
Let us live life to build people, not blast them down with bullets.
Be different for an instant, live for life to be realistic.
I can't stand back and wait, seeing that I've missed it.

I stand before you as me, so let's see.
I know what I am as a man, so reject me.
Hug me, love me, and show me that you care for it.
I've bored torment and I'm glad God was there for it.
Because He showed me love to turn the other cheek.
Instead of trying to retaliate, just to turn the other weak.

He let me be me; he took me as I am.
I learned as I grow into a man.
He was at my birth, He let me survive.
He knows who I am, he left me alive.
He gave me a purpose; he changed me for the better.
I never thought this would happen. Now he's changed me forever.

I see life through the eyes that I've ever seen.
I see right through the lies into a new scene.
I'm given a new life through you, God and I'm grateful.
I know it's all from you, so I stand before you, thankful.
I've seen your face, I won't run from it.

I embrace your love and what comes from it.

I embrace the heart, the art, the love, the walk.
I look for the journey to turn into what I was not.
To live, to give, to see, to hear,
To speak: to be in place right here.
So, how could this all happen in the blink of an eye?
Where you don't hope to die, you just think to the sky.

Now, you see life different for you and those around you.
So, how did this all happen? It's because God has found you.

By My Side

It doesn't matter what's going on, it doesn't matter what we face,
With your strength I can make it through these days, days
I remember when we met; I could never forget it,
As I sit here and think about it, I will never regret it.
We met and became friends; we stood up and stand strong,
I was build up from this; I have a rock to stand on.
See, you came into my life when I had nothing, in fact,
We build each other up, that's why our friendship's intact.
I remember when we used to chill and shoot the breeze in the day,
We were the best of friends, I think of that as your leaving today.
We taught each other of life, you had my back through it all,
With you I can stand, it's because of that I stand tall.
I will continue to walk in it, our friendship doesn't end here.
A friendship that raised me, I will no longer walk in fear.
See, your friendship lifted me, it allowed me to grow,
Now I have a bond that can't break, I just want you to know.

Your friendship means so much to me; of this I am so sure.
You mean so much to me; it all goes by in a blur.
Through the darkest of the dark,
To the lightest of the light,
You stood by my side
And you had my back through the fight.
You have given me strength,
You kept me alive with your might
You continued to love me,
Now we soar to new heights.

It doesn't matter what's going on, it doesn't matter what we face,
With your strength I can make it through these days, days
I never would thought I'd get to the place that I am,
I will walk in the plan that puts us together as we stand.
Now, it's time to let the love of our friendship show as evidence

Of a bond that stands firm and fills the world with decadence.
So, I will hold our bond in my heart as I stand in this life,
I demand to stand right because you've got my back in this fight.
All that I've learned from you and all that you have given me here
Fuels the fire of my life and has allowed me to live without fear.
So, I will take the gifts given and the strength you're provided
And ignite it and light it, there's no possible way I could hide it.
I have been given strength to face all that I face in this race,
I can't be misplaced as long as I look at your face.
You have given me the muscle as I walk in your guidance,
With all that I face, I look to your friendship to forever provide this

And I thank you for walking with me through the years,
I am thankful for the friendship that we have right here.
Through the darkest of the dark,
To the lightest of the light,
You stood by my side
And you had my back through the fight.
You have given me strength,
You kept me alive with your might
You continued to love me,
Now we soar to new heights.

It doesn't matter what's going on, it doesn't matter what we face,
With your strength I can make it through these days, days.
There's not a day where I don't thank God for the friends that I've made,
Every day I am a living testimony, I pray that I never strayed,
If you ever say that you need me, you better believe that I will forever stay,
I will be by your side because you're right by mine; it's you and me together, eh?
So, I going to take this time just to tell you all
I appreciate our time, especially through this all.
I appreciate every battle and even every fall as we walk this out just to hear God's call.
So, I just want to take a second and thank you all for all that you've done,

It's all begun; we've got it started; now it's on the run.
So, just call me when you need me, just know that I'm there.
It doesn't matter what's going on, I just want to blow the sky with new flares.
It's time to take on our enemies with our best friends by our side,
We can't hide, so I will be right with you as the world will collide.
It's time to make each other stronger; it's time to raise the roof.
With you all by my side I can make it through, it's the strength of truth,

And you have given me the strength; it's time to strengthen you.
Through the darkest of the dark,
To the lightest of the light,
You stood by my side
And you had my back through the fight.
You have given me strength,
You kept me alive with your might
You continued to love me,
Now we soar to new heights.

It doesn't matter what's going on, it doesn't matter what we face,
With your strength I can make it through these days, days

Never Knowing What I Will Find

I've been writing for 14 years, man, has it been that long?
I can remember the words I formed, not to mention the million songs,
That I put together just to try to explain what was going wrong.
I always saw myself as weak, I don't know, I guess I'm strong.
I guess it's just hard to tell, so I guess I'll keep strolling on,
And I'll pick up the pen, keep doodling and just scrolling on.
Not sure what to say, so I'll keep writing until the words are drawn,
I write in hopes that they hit in such a way that your hurt is gone.
Now, I form words and sentences in hopes that you will learn to grow,
Becoming what God has intended, allowing God's word to show.
So, I'll pick up my pen, write of His grace, just so that you could know,
Who God is and the love He has, I guess it's time to let it go.
I guess it's time to give it up, so, LORD I give you everything,
I give you the words in my rhymes, the thoughts in my mind, because
you can give me anything.
I am no longer weak; I am strengthened by you, my king,
And I will love you and praise you; it is because of you I sing.

Your words whisper through my mind,
I follow them whole heartedly.
Never knowing what I will find,
I can't just give you a part of me.
I can give you all, hoping to find,
a love that will be guarding me.
As I walk this life of mine,
I seek love that's so far from me.

Now I sit here, pen in hand, and it seems all I can ask,
Let my words follow you for how you've forgotten my past.
Let my life worship you, for who you are, I'm last,
Because all I've seen is your embrace as I continued to walk past.
I don't know what I was looking for, but I just kept wondering.
I wanted the answers to life, so I just kept thinking and pondering,

Thinking I would find the answers one day, it seems I kept dishonoring,
Who you are and how you made me, I wanted something more self-honoring.
I stood weak, acting as if I were truly strong,
Not knowing what strength was because I wasn't seeing you, I was gone.
I was seeking the catacombs of my mind in rhyme, trying to sound tough in song,
But it didn't show that way, it seems ignorance was growing on.
Now I see the truth, I know why I grab the pen,
I grab the pen to strengthen men through God's word, once again,
We can live by His standard and we can teach it to others in the end,
Waiting for Christ to come back and take us to Him again.

Your words whisper through my mind,
I follow them whole heartedly.
Never knowing what I will find,
I can't just give you a part of me.
I can give you all, hoping to find,
A love that will be guarding me,
As I walk this life of mine,
I seek love that's so far from me.

In Psalm 139, verses 23 and 24 it says,
"Search me, God, and know my heart;
Test me and know my anxious thoughts.
See if there is any offensive way in me, and lead me in the way everlasting."
LORD, I pray that these words would be a testimony of how you've searched my heart,
You changed my outlook and my life. Thank you, Father.

My Future Fades

I've tried.
I don't think I can try again.
I've cried.
I don't think I want to cry again.
I've failed.
I don't think I'll ever have that friend.
Oh well,
I'll soak in loneliness and smile in pretend.

I never would have thought this would happen. It seems my life is a blur.
I tried to ensure my happiness, not realizing the emotions that I would stir.
Now, I'm hoping that I can maintain this, but it seems now that I'm not so sure.
I guess I forgot what my aim is because I chose not to see her.
I chose not to let myself feel, waiting until my heart was ready.
I thought I had it together; now I just can't seem to hold it steady.
I want to learn to feel again, but the fear makes my heart heavy.
Now, I can't hold my head up, why do you think I'll hold this relationship steady?
And every day I hear from another their concern over this aspect,
It seems to be on every person's mind, but nobody seems to ask it.
Now, it's become taboo and I fight to continue to mask it.
I don't want the world to know I am this, so I play dumb, I've had it.
I will no longer lay hurt; I will heal from this catastrophe.
I will grow into a better man; lift my head up from this shadow cast on me.
My broken heart will heal; I can't let you set the final cast on me.
I'm on a new stage, my new frame is already racing right past, passing me.

Darkness closes in; it seems I can't see through.
The clouds just surround me, no matter what I do.
I want to smile again, but this doesn't seem real.

My walls protect me because they don't let me feel.
The time has passed; I'm way past ready,
My future fades without my life being steady.
I thought I'd have more by this day and age,
But I won't reach to open up to the next stage.
Because.....

I've tried.
I don't think I can try again.
I've cried.
I don't think I want to cry again.
I've failed.
I don't think I'll ever have that friend.
Oh well,
I'll soak in loneliness and smile in pretend.

Now, I can't say I haven't been burnt; my skin is scorched from the experience.
Now, I can look at what I've learned, no recovering vision, never been as clear as this.
No more blurred vision from tears dripping, but I can't stay steering clear from this.
I know what I've been a part of; now I can only hope you listen when you're hearing this.
All I want to do is be new; it looks as if this pattern's broken.
I've been through this before; I've already felt this sadder emotion.
I think of her daily, not being hear her is the cause of the commotion.
Now, my ignorance shows its ugly head and I drown in your ocean.
I can't swim in your love, I can't even breathe, I wheeze.
It seems I can't see, my walls were built by my own pleads.
I took a stance and became caged. Now I wonder if I'll ever leave.
And if I never leave, will my life be worth it? Will I ever see?
I don't want to listen to myself; I refuse to hear your suggestions.
Not sure what I really want, I guess I never truly learned from the lessons.
I live for approval, but refuse to live due to my own discretion.
I guess I love watching my friends leave, it allows me live in depression.

Darkness closes in; it seems I can't see through.
The clouds just surround me, no matter what I do.
I want to smile again, but this doesn't seem real.
My walls protect me because they don't let me feel.
The time has passed; I'm way past ready,
My future fades without my life being steady.
I thought I'd have more by this day and age,
But I won't reach to open up to the next stage.
Because....

I've tried.
I don't think I can try again.
I've cried.
I don't think I want to cry again.
I've failed.
I don't think I'll ever have that friend.
Oh well,
I'll soak in loneliness and smile in pretend.

I love my friends; I can never forget any of you all.
But it seems that I can't let you see me not stand tall.
I'm alone again the minute I hide in my own walls;
The only thing that's truly mine, the only place I can fall.
I befriend those I can help because I refuse to help myself.
I guess my happiness doesn't matter to me as long as you can smile
yourself.
Now, my loneliness is too heavy to hold steady, it destroys my health,
But I smile on until the trial's gone, I can't let you guys help.
As the days go by, the night's getting darker, I can't stand it.
I let time slide by, I missed the marker even though I plant it.
Now, I can't comprehend it, Why is my life not where I planned it?
By the time I'm old I'll have plenty that I took for granted.
Apparently the choice was too much for me to decide,
Do I make friends or wait then wonder why I'm still on the side?
Now, the real question in my heart must re-occur where I reside:
Can I bring any change or has the opportunity already died?

Darkness closes in; it seems I can't see through.
The clouds just surround me, no matter what I do.
I want to smile again, but this doesn't seem real.
My walls protect me because they don't let me feel.
The time has passed; I'm way past ready,
My future fades without my life being steady.
I thought I'd have more by this day and age,
But I won't reach to open up to the next stage.
Because....

I've tried.
I don't think I can try again.
I've cried.
I don't think I want to cry again.
I've failed.
I don't think I'll ever have that friend.
Oh well,
I'll soak in loneliness and smile in pretend.

Can You Imagine?

My words are empty, but yours are filling.
So, I'm feeling that the feeling they get from you is fulfilling.
So, I pray you would move them, send them in to motion,
Into a whirlwind of emotion that moves coast to coast like an ocean.
So, LORD love them, even though they betray,
Because one day they may say they will love you for all days.
So, anoint us dear Father as we speak your word,
So, we ensure that they love and respect what they've heard,
So, fill us with your presence as we walk in your glory,
A glory that puts us in your arms as you cradle us wholly,

Because your presence is perfect and your love is my life!
Now I'm in love with my life as I learn to walk in your sight.
Now all I can do is learn to grow in your love,
It's the love of the blood that was shed for me from above.
You gave up your kingdom just for the day I would meet you.
Now I need you, please give me the strength just to seek you.
Can you imagine just what goes through my mind when I see you?
There's nothing I say to prove I love you,
But I won't shrug you; I can never put anything above you.

So, LORD takes my life and everything that I've given,
Help me to stay driven as I live the life of the forgiven.
Give me your hand, Father as you strengthen my stance,
You take my trials and my hurt and you gave me a chance.
You let me learn from my mistakes as I place it all in your palms.
From the Gospels to the Psalms, I give you all of my qualms.
Regardless of what we face, regardless of what we see,
Give us strength to face everything that we can be.
So, give us guidance, Father and please allow us to follow,
Please build us up in your grace; I don't want to be hollow.

Let your Word change us, lets us grow in your grace,
Let's trace your face so we can imprint this world with your embrace.
So, let's change this world for a better way,
a way to show love to a world that will save us today.
Can you imagine just what goes through my mind when I see you?
We don't know what to say, we just want to know who you are,
We know you exist, why do you think we look into the stars?
You are our creator, our love, and our life's joy.
So, give us a joy that will allow us fill our soul's void.
Your truth is perfect although we pervert and distort it,
We'll never support it until we see how you're important.

Answer our questions, oh LORD, allow us to get to know you,
So we don't roll through our lives without seeking the whole you.
There's nothing that we can say to get you to believe in us,
But you still lived to love us; you proclaimed you're never leaving us.
And just for that, we owe you our lives, we owe you our being.
We owe you our emceeing and what we're being all because you're freeing.
So, LORD, give us your Word, shows us an undeniable truth,
Show us the same truth that can be used to reach all ages of our youth.
And as we seek into our faith, place your hand in our path,
A path of power that leads us to your grace; turning from your wrath.

Can you imagine just what goes through my mind when I see you?

Break Down The Walls (A Change is Upon Us)

Break down the walls. Break down the doors.
Break down the lifestyle that you call yours.
Let your life change drastically,
So you can keep catching these minds of the generations, who lived this
life bastardly.
May you see a new light of a new life?
May you see a new day and light of new night.
I pray the world change for the better; right now, a new stance.
I pray for a new change, a new stand for a man with a plan for new plans.
So, show us the world; the Good, the bad, the ugly.
And please hug me instead of hurting me, rugby.
Let's change the way we act, instead of copycatting.
Then we'll be genuine and won't let a copy cat in.
Let us learn from men instead of trying to copy cat men,
To the point where we walk backwards and have to step back in.
I mean, what happened to being individual people?
Now, we've gotten to the point where we're individually evil.
Since we act the same, we're individually feeble,
Is this really what we expected from individual people?

Break down the walls, change our lives.
Give us a new rhyme, let us rise.
Let us learn, let us grow.
Give us a new vision that we can show.
A change is upon us, branched through our hearts.
The change is honest, branched through arts.

Let's stand up, let's do what we feel.
Let's keep it real on the field.
Let's change over time, so we're not just reiterating;
Playing the same role over, hoping we're being entertaining.
How can every emcee claim to change the game?
When the game's fame and chains continues to be the same?

How is it that every lyric is the same, a minor variety?
The line will be written a different times because different, no one tries
to be.
All rhymes will be diamonds, rides, drugs, guns?
Are these the rhymes you want used by your sons?
Sex acts, next dance, loving for the dollar?
Is this the kind of lives you want for your daughters?
I know it ain't,
So why would you walk around with such a tainted picture to paint?

Break down the walls, change our lives.
Give us a new rhyme, let us rise.
Let us learn, let us grow.
Give us a new vision that we can show.
A change is upon us, branched through our hearts.
The change is honest, branched through arts.

Tell of Few Tales

I met this young man at the age of ten.
He picked up a pen to release the rage within.
He revealed himself with every rhyme that he wrote.
He never wanted to be dope; he just used it to cope.
You see, I talked to him and he told me a tale.
A tale of his life, he swore he would never tell.
You see, as he grew up he felt shame in his heart.
He went through a change, but it never changed in his heart.
No matter what he did, he felt he was never accepted.
He was never directed; he just felt he'd never accept it.
He told me how he fought for his father's approval,
But he never seemed to get it, in despair he thought of removal.
He wanted to be removed from his family, removed from the Earth.
God gave him a gift, but he saw it as a curse.
We sat on the steps; a tear came to his eye.
He grabbed his notebook and told me he was ready to die.

The years went by, pain deepened within him.
He looked for the better, but found nothing within him.
He kept writing secretly in his room,
His heart came out, dark and grey in the gloom.
He tried to show his hurt to the people he knew,
But their ears were closed, the words never made it through.
So, he hid his words, becoming ashamed of what he wrote.
Trying to fit in with his friends, knowing he did what they don't.
You see, they're friends, but his left at a distance.
He tries to keep up, but he fears there's a difference.
They begin to have girlfriends, jobs and cars.
He moves away to college but he won't move so far.
He stays the same, he stays trapped in himself.
He keeps writing, hoping he will adapt to himself.
We sat at the table, his notebook in his hand.
He learned that through God he will be made to a man.

We sat at the table, we both waited to speak.
Silence fell between us as we nervously tapped a beat.
I told him the grace of God, he fumbles through his notes.
I had my Bible in hand, desperately thinking of some quotes.
He looked up at me, a gleam of shame in his eye.
He couldn't faith in God, but he didn't know why.
He said he believed, but couldn't express it in the open.
He felt the eyes of man and his attention was broken.
He listened to the sermons and the songs that they sang.
He saw they weren't ashamed and he wanted the same.
He buried his head, he eyed the floor.
I told him that in God you can have so much more.
Over time as you learn and follow his word,
You will learn to be yourself, forgetting your nerves.
I looked into his eyes as I repeated the name.
He learned that through Him, he will finally be unashamed.

Untitled

I'm not coming back from a break, there is no sabbatical.
You don't know the steps I will take; I guess I 'm just a radical.
You can try to divide the stakes, but I am not mathematical.
I will not act as the fakes; they will be thrown by my catapult.
You could never see how I'm consumed by my consumption,
I know the world is fallen; I don't need to assume there's corruption.
I am waiting for the rapture; I will be taken up like abduction.
My Father is building a kingdom; He's the head of this construction.
So, I guess the time has come for us to stand like a statue,
Let His word attack you, just know that we will do whatever we have to,
To get you to hear the Word, we're here to serve even if we gas you,
And even when we get you mad about the Truth, we will follow just like
Matthew.
(Matthew 5:11)

And we will take steps into His path, even if it leads us to persecution.
There's no illusion, we know that only God can heal the ruined.
So, let's speak the Truth and tell all what God is doing,
Even if we're hated, we know that this should be heard by all humans.
It's time to condense the lyrics, turn them into a compact,
It's time create a bomb rap that mirrors an image like looking into a
compact.
I am on that, on track, that allows my words to run to your ears making
contact,
And it all runs through your brains and paints a picture of perfection
like using contacts.
My lyrical status will lead to lyrical paralysis,
Your malice is wasted on debate and analysis.
And you lose your chance while I work and gain calluses,
Now the challenge is to use those new experiences to give the world
challenges,
That will allow Man to grow, now that's what true talent is.

You see, I will not leave this game and be nameless,
But my name is etched in His fame, why do you think I want him famous?
The game is aimless, no aim; there's nothing to contain this.
So, my aim is to tell the story of a man who lived life stainless.
He gave us chances after chances to advance this,
Now his hand is our advances to take these stances,
To live for Him, now how will you answer when you find His matchless?
See, the world is crumbling, fumbling over themselves, not looking for covering.
The substance is gone; I'm only left with something so blubbery,
See, I know I'm broken and there's nothing that can ever cover me,
It looks like I needed to relapse, enter rehab just to reach recovery.

Now, I speak the Word, let it emerge verbally.
I turn words to see if you'll reach for the stars, a true hyperbole.
You're not burning me, He removed sin surgically,
I will not fall and I will not show any courtesy.
I have a purpose in life, you can't do all that I can,
Living this life for only one cause; standing as I stand.
You see, I 'm not in the forefront, I guess I'm the hype man.
So, I'll step out; walk on water, while you stay on the dry land.
See, I could create many alter-egos, and name each one of them,
Have each one of them run from Him, saying life is no fun with Him,
They could live their whole lives hoping nothing will be done to them,
But my fame comes from Him, so I want to be seen as one with Him.

Voiceless

The further one dives into their Christian faith, the more action one tends to show their faith. As people who were once voiceless, they now have a voice. As one develops their voice, they begin to gather an understanding of the source of their pain, and then they can better understand the source of their healing.

As I grew as a person, a Christian and a writer/poet, I began to understand that I lived most of my life voiceless. The idea of sharing my opinion or being a leader amongst my friends was illusive to me. I didn't understand it. Yet, I learned that I was not the only person without a voice, therefore I decided to write for the voiceless, hopefully giving them a voice of honesty. That is the context of this collection of poems/songs.

My aim was to share my experience as I learn to gain my voice and share another level of my story. Through this collection I journey further through my brokenness and my guilt. By sharing this, I hope to give truth to those who also share in my brokenness, who feel as if they are broken and also to give them the words to speak when crying out to God.

In the times of our brokenness, when we feel like we have nothing left, we must remember that we still have a voice. That means that we can still call out to God and turn our hearts and our lives over to Him who can save us. When we turn to God to save us, we are given an opportunity to be renewed by the Spirit and created to be something new.

This collection shows that journey that many go through as they grow through their Christian walk, especially as they move through the varied stages of adolescent life into the live of an adult, dealing with adult issues of the heart, mind, body and soul.

Voiceless

We will be heard! We will speak!
We will stand up! We will seek!
We will be heard! We will speak!
We will stand up! We will seek!

It's time for me to speak, no, I'm not voiceless.
I've got no secrets to keep; it's time to voice this.
I'm in a sea that's so deep, I'm surrounded by choices.
But to listen to God speak, that's what my choice is.

I was born voiceless, I could barely speak.
My heart burned, I had secrets I was forced to keep.
It couldn't show, I just hoped the pain wouldn't seep
Into my face, into my life, into my hearts steady beat.
I am who I am, it's because of God I am not weak.
That's why.....

We will be heard! We will speak!
We will stand up! We will seek!
We will be heard! We will speak!
We will stand up! We will seek!

It's time for me to speak, no, I'm not voiceless.
I've got no secrets to keep; it's time to voice this.
I'm in a sea that's so deep, I'm surrounded by choices.
But to listen to God speak, that's what my choice is.

When we speak, it will strike like lightening.
You're fighting, trying not to be frightened.
With every rhyme we touch, every rhyme we bust,
The thyme grabs your attention, turning your attention to us.
We will be seen, our faces will not be faceless,
Our voices will ring in your ears; let's see if you can face this?

The darkness will be brought into the light,
And our words are cocked, locked and loaded, ready to strike.

We will be heard! We will speak!
We will stand up! We will seek!
We will be heard! We will speak!
We will stand up! We will seek!

It's time for me to speak, no, I'm not voiceless.
I've got no secrets to keep; it's time to voice this.
I'm in a sea that's so deep, I'm surrounded by choices.
But to listen to God speak, that's what my choice is.

We are not voiceless, let our voice ring.
Should to the heavens and the message we bring.
We can speak for the voiceless, we give them a voice.
They can speak for others, we give them a choice.
We will give strength to the weak every time we speak.
We will not stay silent, no, we will forever compete.
And when it's done and over, what will we gain?
We'll have voices to speak of and honor His name.
That's why.....

We will be heard! We will speak!
We will stand up! We will seek!
We will be heard! We will speak!
We will stand up! We will seek!

It's time for me to speak, no, I'm not voiceless.
I've got no secrets to keep; it's time to voice this.
I'm in a sea that's so deep, I'm surrounded by choices.
But to listen to God speak, that's what my choice is.

I Should Have Been Better

The struggle continues, the hustle is getting hard.
I struggle when I continue to hurt you with total disregard.
Your heart and soul was given to me so I can stand.
But I continue to fall away, I just don't understand.
I see the nails in your hand, the whips on your back.
The cross that you carried, what more can I ask?
I am a slave to my sins, so I can't be of the spirit.
I am falling apart from within; I pray you can clear it.
I pray that you help me, put me on the track that you know.
I pray that you have been better, please help me to do so!
Please give me your words, help me to the meaning to
The words that you speak; you've showed me what I mean to you.

All I can say is...
I should have been better.
All I know is....
I should have been better.
All I can think is...
I should have been better.

Lord, I am sorry for the way I've been acting,
I know I can change if it's your love I am after.
So, I search and I pray that I know what is happening.
But I have to have faith in your pace; I can't make it go any faster.
Because it is your love for that I am sure,
But I am stuck with my pain; I am stuck with my sin.
Is this the kind of pain that I have to endure?
(All I have to say is....)
God, I need your love, I need your grace.
Can you help me find my way through the race?
Can you give me strength? Can you help me through?
Because all I ever wanted was to see you.
But I fall away, but I know that your love is true.

All I can say is...
I should have been better.
All I know is....
I should have been better.
All I can think is...
I should have been better.

And for all my family and friends that I've hurt over time,
I pray that God's word seeps into my heart and my mind.
Please help me just to seek and then find,
As I continue to see who I can be, to better this time.
I know I've hurt feelings and that I've lied in the past.
I pray for forgiveness and that my family lasts.
Because I never meant to hit them! I never meant to curse!
I never meant to let them down! I should have put you first!
I should have followed your lead! I should have read every letter!
And now I see my consequences and I should have been better!

All I can say is...
I should have been better.
All I know is....
I should have been better.
All I can think is...
I should have been better.

Where Will I Go?

Where will I go? I go? I go? I go?
Where will I go? I go? I go? I go?
Where will I go? I go? I go? I go?
Where will I go? I go? I go? I go?
Where will I go? I go? I go? I go?
Where will I go? I go? I go? I go?

Where will I go in the end?
Will I break the trend or break and bend, trying to mend?
What will I see in the future, can I predict it?
And if I never had it, could you really miss it?
Will you know what you're missing when you hear it?
Do you have to see it, live it, or just have your grasp go near it?
Can my father learn to be a man as he stands in an unplanned plan?
Or does he have to meet a man to see a man to fully understand?
Will he be able to change? Will he be able to see his wrong doing?
Or are we all just stuck in this world through our wrong doing?
I guess all I can ask is.....

Where will I go? I go? I go? I go?
Where will I go? I go? I go? I go?
Where will I go? I go? I go? I go?
Where will I go? I go? I go? I go?
Where will I go? I go? I go? I go?
Where will I go? I go? I go? I go?

What will I see continuing my journey?
Will I help people? Or watch them hurt each other, eternal burning?
Can I change lives from what I've learned?
Can I make them see they are truly valued from what we've earned?
Can I break the pattern of my family tree?
Or am I a boat, trying to float in this insanity sea?
Or can I change their minds, showing what exactly Christianity be?

Can I change how I live?
Will I be able to share what I did?
I guess I'll never know,
All I can ask is where will I go?

Where will I go? I go? I go? I go?
Where will I go? I go? I go? I go?
Where will I go? I go? I go? I go?
Where will I go? I go? I go? I go?
Where will I go? I go? I go? I go?
Where will I go? I go? I go? I go?

Will I see the end? Will I see how it happened?
Do I have the power to free my family from the cage they're trapped in?
I May not, but how would I know if I don't try it?
I lay it before them, hoping they're like it.
It's time to break the trend, how's it been?
Re-write the beginning, middle, and end.
It's time to help them up. It's time to watch them grow.
Look up to the heavens, so you don't have to ask where I'll go.

Where will I go? I go? I go? I go?
Where will I go? I go? I go? I go?
Where will I go? I go? I go? I go?
Where will I go? I go? I go? I go?
Where will I go? I go? I go? I go?
Where will I go? I go? I go? I go?

I Call Out

We fell apart; I never thought this would be.
What did I do to have this happen to me?
What can I do to see this thing through?
When the only man I seem to love and hate is you?
How can I see myself when you don't see?
How you see yourself reflects on me?
I'm sorry I'm not perfect, but wait.....
Is this really what you saw as your fate?
Follow the trail because God has a plan;
For your breath, heart, head, hand.
Give yourself to him, please,
Because he hears your cries and pleads,
To give you life, the reasons he bleeds.
I know that it can be hard
When you are only left with scabs and scars,
But follow the lobe in your heart
And you will go far.

I call out,
But you don't seem to listen.
I fall out,
But you don't save me.
I pray for you, hoping it makes effect.
I pray for you, asking God, "What's next?"
I pray for you, hoping this can't be real.
I pray for you, knowing you can be healed.
I know you've been through things, what can I say?
I know that for you I continuously pray.
I ask God to give you a hand with the pain in your life,
Know that He can come through; just follow the image of Christ.

I'm Done!

It ain't about where you came from. It's about where you are with it.
So, if you live a mellow life, there's no need to be hard with it.
Just go hard with it and make sure there's no hard in it.
Put your heart in it, write from the soul.
Feel what you feel, just don't feel you lose control.
See, I came from a drug family, where the pain could be in endlessness.
But I'll look to the future, there's no need to reminisce.
I'm just ending this, no need to keep sending this.
This is the end of this, forget the trend in this.

I'm done with the past and ready for the present.
I'm ready for the present, knowing that life is a present.
I'm done with what's done and I'm ready for what's to come.
But what's to come, no one knows till your time is done.

I've got a heart of gold and daily speak through it.
I keep true; it's a problem when I keep to it.
I fight to keep my head up, I write when I'm fed up.
Don't let up. Everyday I've got to get up.
But what can I do when I'm discouraged? No courage.
The words settle me down; try to head me toward a new verge.
The words settle me down; when I stand as a man where I am.
Where I can be, just lay out a plan.

I'm done with the past and ready for the present.
I'm ready for the present, knowing that life is a present.
I'm done with what's done and I'm ready for what's to come.
But what's to come, no one knows till your time is done.

Now I could let the pain devour me, shower me to be cowardly.
So, how could we live with this and it not sour me?
Now, the world can crush upon my shoulders and I'll hold till I get older.
Never let it break me, never let it smolder.

Now, there's times when I get burned,
The burn turns into a lesson in depression and I forever learn.
Now, I'm here, waiting, looking for the next turn.

I'm done with the past and ready for the present.
I'm ready for the present, knowing that life is a present.
I'm done with what's done and I'm ready for what's to come.
But what's to come, no one knows till your time is done.

Change

How could I-grow up without knowing,
Who I am? Who I'll see? What I'll be? I'm not showing,
Any improvement in my eyes, but I am,
I am child, I'm a son, I'm a brother, and I'm a man.
Man, I can't see tomorrow.
Today's looking better when yesterday gave me nothing but sorrow.
It gave me nothing but pain, insane.
It's all the same. I'm just a player in this world and this world's a game.
All I do is wrong, at least so I thought,
The only thing I do well is all that I'm taught.
I teach, who I lead, who I reach
Taught to reach in this world I don't preach.
I learn, tell and give lessons.
Not understanding it all, but still trying to make a good impression.
But it's hard when you don't know who you are,
Because the world we live in's so bizarre. It's hard.

There's a lot that I can't see.
The world trying to change me to whom I'll be.
There's not a lot I can do.
Either change into me or turn into you.
There's not a lot that I can say.
I love living life, but I want to be taken away. (Taken away)
I can't see who I am.
As long as I grow up to be a normal man.
What else could I be?
Be changed and re-arranged, I will not be. (Not be)

I see the world through the vision of invisible precision.
Living in this world hating every minute I'm missing.
Not sure why I'm here. Am I here on a mission?
Am I here to be the person everyone isn't?
Well, if I am than man, how does that make me a man?

Do I grow at my own pace? Living in my own land?
Can I expand my thoughts and feelings?
No longer concealing just revealing, hoping one day I'll keep building.
On everything that I knew,
The old, the new, alone, the crew, alone we grew.
What can I do? But just continue,
Not sure who we were or who we'll turn into.
We venue: hoping to change the world that we're into.

There's a lot that I can't see.
The world trying to change me to whom I'll be.
There's not a lot I can do.
Either change into me or turn into you.
There's not a lot that I can say.
I love living life, but I want to be taken away. (Taken away)
I can't see who I am.
As long as I grow up to be a normal man.
What else could I be?
Be changed and re-arranged, I will not be. (Not be)

How do I explain a life that you don't completely understand?
When the demands you demand me to be a certain man.
And you're not sure how you can complete his wishes,
And still be you. It seems the world is so vicious.
Then, you find out find out it's not the world, just him.
Now, you look at the world differently, it's hard to trust him.
It's not his fault, that's all he knows.
He learns these lessons by himself as he thrives and grows.
See, every man must grow and learn on his own.
No one can help, just hope you find your way home.
We're all alone, fighting
Hoping we're doing right when we're writing.
The enlightening of the fighting teaches us about life and
We learn of the pain of the people and the evil that's rising.
Every day we hope it will end, when it won't
Unsure who we are as humans, we grab for the throat.

Will we cope with the change?
Can we cope with range of people of the world? Can we cope with the strange and deranged?
When will life change?

There's a lot that I can't see.
The world trying to change me to whom I'll be.
There's not a lot I can do.
Either change into me or turn into you.
There's not a lot that I can say.
I love living life, but I want to be taken away. (Taken away)
I can't see who I am.
As long as I grow up to be a normal man.
What else could I be?
Be changed and re-arranged, I will not be. (Not be)

In This Life I Cannot Dwell.

I could have fallen to pieces,
But I thought of a new thesis.
Where all the pain releases:
It releases in the Holy name of Jesus.
I could have been devoured,
When I'm only seen as a coward,
Where life could have been soured,
But I chose to be empowered.
Now, I will never be broken,
Never be stuck without coping,
I'm not brining false thought and false hope in.
NO! In God's light I will soak in.
I stand before you, God!
I can't ignore you, God!
In this life I cannot dwell,
God, you pulled me out of hell.
I could have been trapped,
I could be running through the same race, same laps.
I'm just waiting to collapse,
But I'm living in God's grasp.
I was born and raised a sinner,
Torn and engraved no winner.
My heart; cold and grey like winter,
But in you, God, I'm a new beginner.
Now I stand at your feet,
I'm just waiting for you to speak.
You give me strength I am not weak.
I just pray that my promise I will keep.....
I stand before you, God!
I can't ignore you, God!
In this life I cannot dwell,
God, you pulled me out of hell.

Save me!

I've got a problem growing beneath me
My growing, it's beastly.
My heart's not where the beast be.
LORD, please don't let them reach me.
Because every day I look into my heart and I know there's good in it.
But how could it get easier for me to get what I want to get,
When it's something I know I shouldn't get.
But I go down the path constantly, it conquers me.
So, consciously I guess I don't know where my conscience be.
It's time to destroy the monstrosity.
(So I ask) Can I really be a man of the LORD?
Rose to live out the plan of the LORD?
When I don't quite understand the accord?
I try to stand for Him, but I'm constantly floored.
(All because) the depth my heart falls into the depth of the dark,
Sets fall apart bringing negative effect to the art. (So I say...)

Save me! (Save me!)
Save me from myself. The person I've become.
Save me! (Save me!)
Change what I am; help me live for your son.
Save me! (Save me!)
I try to stand up, but I fall and I stumble.
Save me! (Save me!)
I want to raise a man up, so I try to stay humbled.

I'm looking into a mirror.
My face distorted with fear.
Thinking the answers will never be clear.
What am I doing here?
I try to be the man, who lives his life with respect,
But I neglect to respect the women I should have sworn to protect.
(But instead) I'm trapped inside of this trap,

I'm trapped where I interact with the internet pack.
I try to react, but I just fall and relapse.
Now, I am ready to get rid of these laps,
I'm putting my problems under wraps.
(So now,) I bow and pray for forgiveness,
To the women that I hurt when I sat and I lived this.
(I pray) As I live and I grow,
I know that there is more that women can show.
(I see) There is more to them than body frames,
They're built beautiful when they live in the frame of His Godly name.
(So I ask) That God changes me for good,
Allowing me to be better, I want to be what I should.
So I ask that He.....

Save me! (Save me!)
Save me from myself. The person I've become.
Save me! (Save me!)
Change what I am; help me live for your son.
Save me! (Save me!)
I try to stand up, but I fall and I stumble.
Save me! (Save me!)
I want to raise a man up, so I try to stay humbled.

I fuel my sin with lust and frolic eyes,
It's all in lies that fill lives with solid lies.
I call in cries, calling for solid ties,
So, to these women, I apologize.
In Him I wasn't entrusting,
I was thrusting myself into the women's body, the object of my lusting.
(I know) My words don't heal the wounds when I conceal the tombs.
I feel the gloom for your image, So, I pray that we kill the doom.
Let's create an image of love,
And in it the love will begin above, so we can begin it in love.
(Because) We are falling from the graces.
In the places he placed us to love all His creations.
How can we embrace this if our face is traced in sin in our relations?

So I ask....

Save me! (Save me!)
Save me from myself. The person I've become.
Save me! (Save me!)
Change what I am; help me live for your son.
Save me! (Save me!)
I try to stand up, but I fall and I stumble.
Save me! (Save me!)
I want to raise a man up, so I try to stay humbled.

I Will Love

I thought of you today, and I didn't know what to say.
I just know I love you and I will every day.
I can't even explain it, words can't describe,
What you mean to me, I cannot lie.
I will fight for you because your love is worthy.
Your grace is grand; I know you would never hurt me.
I would never dream of causing you pain,
I will walk in love, simply because you came.
With you came change in this walk of life,
I will treasure you simply because you're my delight.
Every single day, regardless of what we've seen,
We will be together, standing as a team.
I am so thankful for you, can't take you for granted.
Every day I'll be happy with the roots we've planted.
So, let's keep digging, no longer waiting,
I will love you through it all, love it not fading.

I've got this opportunity to love you night and day.
I can't wait to love you more, that is all I'd like to say.
Your beauty's radiant, your love feels my life with joy.
I want to give my all to you; your love's what I enjoy.
What more can I do? You gave me yourself.
I will protect your love, I ask God for help.
I know that with your love, I'm not by myself.
I will protect your love, I ask God for help.

I just wanted you to know I'm praying for you daily.
No matter what we face, I'm in love with what you gave me.
I can't wait to stand, everyday hand in hand,
Without knowing you, I could never know who I am.
And I promise to love you simply for loving me,
And I will keep you strong because of what you've done for me.
So, let me stand before you, no longer hurt by my past,

We will grow together, I will not lose grasp.
I will love you from now on from this day forth.
I want to treat you right, so I can no longer walk my course.
I want to treat my life as yours, nothing else will do,
No longer contaminated because that's what I need this man to do.
I do not look at your past because our future's bright.
We will live our life to show the light of Christ.
So, I will love you greatly because He loved us greatly,
Our hearts are one. You're the one that God gave me.

I've got this opportunity to love you night and day.
I can't wait to love you more, that is all I'd like to say.
Your beauty's radiant, your love feels my life with joy.
I want to give my all to you; your love's what I enjoy.
What more can I do? You gave me yourself.
I will protect your love, I ask God for help.
I know that with your love, I'm not by myself.
I will protect your love, I ask God for help.

I'm a Teacher

I'm a teacher. I'm a parent.
I'm a person. It's apparent,
Life can't get any better till I try to dare it.
I'm a human. I'm a sinner.
I'm a loser. I'm a winner.
How can we warm up to each when our heart is winter?

It's time for a change, but where will the change occur?
Can it happen in our homes or our relationships over?
Can we learn from our parents when they don't set an example?
Can they learn from us, or are we both a handful?
Can we change how we live? Will life then get better?
Or are we stuck in the pattern, where we will be forever?
How can I follow the rules, the rules that I've set?
Can I be my own person or am I doomed to follow the set?
Do I need to follow their expectations? Feel boxed in their bubble?
Can I be who I am, or will my personality get me into trouble?

I'm a teacher. I'm a parent.
I'm a person. It's apparent,
Life can't get any better till I try to dare it.
I'm a human. I'm a sinner.
I'm a loser. I'm a winner.
How can we warm up to each when our heart is winter?

It's time for a change and it can only come with a choice.
We can work with our hands and we can speak with our voice.
Our relationships can build and break the pattern that we lived.
It's only if we don't yield and show the love we can give.
So, you can be a teacher, a parent of a child,
And still be a change to the world with a smile.
Or you can be a teen, who refuses to follow a crowd,
And you can blaze a new trail while you stand proud.

Fight for your sight, regardless of the situation.
Rise up! Never let a low position determine your determination.

I'm a teacher. I'm a parent.
I'm a person. It's apparent,
Life can't get any better till I try to dare it.
I'm a human. I'm a sinner.
I'm a loser. I'm a winner.
How can we warm up to each when our heart is winter?

So, with the little actions and with the minor jobs,
We can raise a church, we can live for God.
We don't have to follow patterns; we create our own paths,
Allowing others to walk behind us, we can re-configure math.
So, live for the moment, God will take you far.
In Him, no one is weak, no matter how strong you are.
So, take your first step, the direction has already been pointed.
You were made for this moment, you should never feel disjointed.
So, you can be a teacher, a parent, a person, its apparent;
Life can only change with the love, if we share it.

I'm a teacher. I'm a parent.
I'm a person. It's apparent,
Life can't get any better till I try to dare it.
I'm a human. I'm a sinner.
I'm a loser. I'm a winner.
How can we warm up to each when our heart is winter?

You see, only through God can our lives change.
And it don't matter the money you've got, or the place that you are at;
The only thing that matters is that love that you show.
We need to show the love of God, His grace, his power.
Only He can change us, but He chooses to use us for his mission.
I pray we walk in Him. Show the love He has given.

What Do You See?

When you look into the mirror, what do you see?
If you see a sea of beauty and what the world can be,
Then you see who you are and who you can be.
Then you see who how you've been saved, been set free.
When you look into the mirror, what do you notice?
If you notice a notice that can grow us the closest,
Then you notice the focus of the world and it's hopeless,
Then you notice the focus to show us what hope is.
When you look into the mirror, you see the individual.
The individuality isn't just visual; it goes deeper than what's visible.
It goes into our thoughts and words as we grow lyrical.
So, let's not be critical. Let's not make them miserable.
Because you were born unique, you were created by hands,
That molds you into creation and you're placed in the plan.
You were given a life that extends and expands.
So, let's light up the days by just living life grand.

When you look into the mirror, what do you see? See? See? See?
When you look into your heart, what do you see? See? See? See?
When you look into yourself, what do you see? See? See? See?
Well, when you look I hope you see how special you are to me.

When you look into a mirror, do you see life's gift?
Do you see a gift that exists through the eyes of God's ifs?
Do you see a gift that exists without lies and no rifts?
Do you see a gift that equips our lives to love this? (life)
Because life is a gift and your presence isn't an accident.
So, use your talent to better the world, let's change the acts in it.
Let's show the youngsters how to live, put faith and facts in it.
Then we can change the world but our continual acts in it.
You see, only you can affect the world with the gifts you've been given.
It is the essence of life that keeps us continually driven.
It is the lives we affect that direct the life we are living.

So, affect lives as only you can, leaving them positively smitten.
So, how can you affect lives with the life that you lead?
You can either with the art on your walls or writing the book that we read.
Or you can by having a love for children, wanting to watch them succeed.
Either way you want to do it, let your presence be freed.

When you look into the mirror, what do you see? See? See? See?
When you look into your heart, what do you see? See? See? See?
When you look into yourself, what do you see? See? See? See?
Well, when you look I hope you see how special you are to me.

You see, you are one of a kind with something special to offer.
You gave your heart and your mind and become a new author,
To the new thoughts and a new story that you build and you foster,
That can reconstruct the world and this life that we offer.
Because you were born with a gift and you live for a purpose.
So, show the world what you are; let it go deeper than the surface.
Let it plant seed and take root, let it grow deep in your verses,
You can set an example of purity in the world full of curses.
You see, you are unique from your fingers to your eyes,
To your desires, to your speech, to the thoughts you realize,
You're unique to your breath, to your heart beat. Together it all ties
Into the gifts that is you; a gift that's hard to disguise.
Now, when you look into the mirror, is it you that you see?
Do you see who you are and who you are meant to be?
If you do, I pray you use it to change the world that we see
Because only you are who you are and that it who you should be,

When you look into the mirror, what do you see? See? See? See?
When you look into your heart, what do you see? See? See? See?
When you look into yourself, what do you see? See? See? See?
Well, when you look I hope you see how special you are to me.

Keep Your Eyes on Me

I know you want me to stop, you need me to quit,
I can't slip! I've got to tighten the strength of my grip.
You expected me to fall, but I can't, I'm too equipped;
I'm equipped from the breath in the lungs to the words from the lips.
So, spread rumors on how what I do doesn't matter,
Your chitter-chatter shatters when the truth starts to lather.
The growth of a person is why I do this, so step up to the plate, batter.
May my voice be like thunder; your reign is tiny pitter patter.
I will not fight for respect; I'll let my work do the talking,
I'm not stopping, I'll keep walking through it all, keep mocking.
I don't even seek revenge; let's pull a grip over ourselves.
No need to destroy self-respect due to other's bad wealth.
That doesn't mean I'll keep quiet while the world falls apart.
The time has come to make noise, not just hide it in art.
My personal life will match my public, no need for flip-flopping.
This is me, so what you see is what you get, got it?

Keep your eyes on me.
See what I'm doing.
Watch what my next step is,
Know what I'm pursuing.
Talk your talk,
Don't forget to engrave and save it.
Since talk is cheap,
Why do we continue to make the payment?
Watch me, Watch me;
Notice me if you must.
You can't stop me, stop me.
Show trust within me when I know I bust.
Keep your eyes on me.
Keep your eyes on me.

I know you expected me to be false, not authentic.
But reset your setting because I'm taking expectations to wreck it.
Project it, you can't dismantle the way I direct it.
Goal one: entertain. Goal two: life effected.
So, give me the word, I'm ready to make a wake.
I don't fake the weight, only guide the words I spake.
So, go ahead and speculate, let the rumors start in.
Spark them because when it comes to real truth, you never even harken.
Confusion wrestles in, muddling the mind of the believer.
Now your life is compromised and the lies burn like a fever.
And I can't say I haven't been burnt, my skin's scorched from the experience.
Now I can look at what I've learned, no recovering, vision's never been as clear as this.
I am thankful for my past, every little bit that brought me here.
I'm thankful to be in a place of grace, triumphant because you're here.
So, go ahead and don't love me, take my life and put hate on it.
Unravel the scroll and unroll the roll of Slim Shady comparisons and see how I rate on it.

Keep your eyes on me.
See what I'm doing.
Watch what my next step is,
Know what I'm pursuing.
Talk your talk,
Don't forget to engrave and save it.
Since talk is cheap,
Why do we continue to make the payment?
Watch me, Watch me;
Notice me if you must.
You can't stop me, stop me.
Show trust within me when I know I bust.
Keep your eyes on me.
Keep your eyes on me.

You may think I fell off; I've been hoisted back into position;

Sit and listen and see if you don't understand my job description.

Let your mind roam through theories while I verbally destroy the song's verse.

You're on first with no audience, so you can just rap at your shoes, Converse.

While I rhyme I am ready to make your ears perk open,

No perverse joking, just pure rhymes that leaves your thirst soaking.

You can look like you're starving, just know that you're thirst has been quenched.

With fine rhymes there's no wet whistle, it's like your flute has been drenched.

Let me guess, I'm a Christian I'm not meant to rap so fiercely.

Try to throw your sharpest tongue at me, but still your words won't pierce me.

So, say whatever you need to say just to soften the blows,

Talk to your foes; just understand that I'm here to impose.

I'll throw you off your balancing act while you teeter totter your understanding.

This is not a play place, so stop fooling around with your underhand standing.

Dirty deeds deal with dirty dealings,

That's why hurt hearts love continually hurting feelings.

The Eternal Rabbit Hole

Throughout my Christian walk I went through a variety of trials that I depended on God's guidance to lead me through these difficult moments, but what happens when I step away from my faith and try to walk through this life on my own understanding? The answer: Chaos!

From 2014 to the year of 2016 I struggled with my faith, even leaving my beliefs for something new; potential love. I was looking for a romantic love as well as the love of a promising career. Yet, the more I journeyed through these new adventures the more I realized that I was hurting. I poured so much of my energy into a relationship that was unintentionally pulling me away from God. I was trying to develop a connection with someone I cared for, yet I found myself hurting in the process.

In this time I also was looking at starting my new career as a teacher, a career that I had been planning out for many years. For about a four to five year period I was teaching, but I was not successful nor was I happy. I was miserable.

By pouring my energy into a failing relationship and an unfulfilling career I was left with very little. I was deeply depressed and unsatisfied with my life and the unwavering fact that I left my faith for this life was weighing me down.

I began to ask questions. I found that too often discovering the solutions to the questions that I was asking was leading to further questions that needed to be answered; an eternal rabbit hole of questions.

This collection of songs/poems is those very questions that I was asking and the answers that occupied them. I realized that you will discover many potential answers to the questions that you may ask as you go through depression, but there is only one answer that will fulfill you; your faith in God!

As the questions are asked and the answers are brought to light, I realized that I couldn't answer them all. I could only trust the God that loved me and I could only depend on God to reveal the mysteries of this world to me.

I have begun to trust in God even more now. I am venturing out into a new career and I am uncertain of what is ahead, yet I trust that God will not leave my side as I write and tell stories that tell any who will listen who God is in my life.

The truth is: People are not meant to live this life alone. We are not meant to try to understand all of life's challenges without guidance. What better source to learn from then God when it comes to learning about the world that we live in.

The Eternal Rabbit Hole

Questions run through my mind,
The answers are hard to find.
With every answer discovered
There is another mystery that is left uncovered.
The truth transfigures our lives to the core
Leading to the point to where we're not the same anymore.
Our heartbeat sounds differently from inside of our chest,
We can't understand it until we're at rest.
But it seems we don't rest until the facts are concrete.
We restlessly compete to know the fate that we meet.

So, we fight and we scrap until our knuckles are bloody;
Our breath is gone; the thing keeping us standing is the foundation is muddy.
Now, let that sink in.....
We give thanks daily for the life we take for granted.
We can't stand it when we fail due to the fact that we're not planted.
We float though life adrift in the mystery.
We trail down the rabbit hole in misery,
Searching for the joy we can't describe visually.
Now, we walk through the darkest corridor and light is our only option.
We try to find answers to the deepest questions as we're coughing.
We fight and we struggle, just to get a glimpse;
A glimpse of who we really are, what we've been through inch by inch.

Who Am I?

We give thanks daily for the life we take for granted.
We can't stand it when we fail due to the fact that we're not planted.
We float though life adrift in the mystery.
We trail down the rabbit hole in misery,
Searching for the joy we can't describe visually.
Now, we walk through the darkest corridor and light is our only option.
We try to find answers to the deepest questions as we're coughing.
We fight and we struggle, just to get a glimpse
A glimpse who we really are and what we've been through inch by inch.

The more I walk, the more I learn.
I cannot stop. It's now my turn.
I ask my questions and more return.
Now, my next lesson is to discern.
But now I'm fallen and I'm in the dark.
It's you I'm calling. I need a spark.
Now, what I need is some more heart.
I lay here bleeding. I won't depart.

All I can ask: Who am I?

Let's walk down the path not sure of our destination.
We're breathing on respiration, hoping to see the true image we're chasing.
I thought I had it figured out. The map was set and memorized.
I then realized I lost my way because of a pair of tender eyes.
I'm so deep inside this rabbit hole; I'm rabid and I can't control....
My heart or myself, I need help to leave this rancid soul.
I thought I saw the light inside; now I'm living here fighting pride.
The path I took just showed I died and the faith in my hand was pried...
Out of my grasp and the Devil laughed, but I couldn't pass no matter how hard I tried.

The more I walk, the more I learn.
I cannot stop. It's now my turn.
I ask my questions and more return.
Now, my next lesson is to discern.
But now I'm fallen and I'm in the dark.
It's you I'm calling. I need a spark.
Now, what I need is some more heart.
I lay here bleeding. I won't depart.

All I can ask: Who am I?

I walk solemnly through, not sure what is false or what is true.
Can my heart be renewed without truly changing my view?
With every step that I take, will the sky begin to change hue?
Will I learn something to know to replace something that I knew?
The darkness is comfortable, but the lit path gives sight.
Now, I guess I must choose which path will be right.
There's no right answer, there's only the choice of insight.
So, now I might think with hindsight while the future's in flight.
I have got to chase it at night with my source as my light.

The more I walk, the more I learn.
I cannot stop. It's now my turn.
I ask my questions and more return.
Now, my next lesson is to discern.
But now I'm fallen and I'm in the dark.
It's you I'm calling. I need a spark.
Now, what I need is some more heart.
I lay here bleeding. I won't depart.

All I can ask: Who am I?

Please help to see my heart when my path gets dark.
Help me to be the part that I will need to be when my journey starts.
Will I forget all of my remarks when I have nothing left in my broken heart?

Will I be devoured and remembered as a coward in my final hour?
Can I be showered while I sit in my mind, caked in my tower?
My attitude is sour from the pain I encountered. Can I be empowered?

The more I walk, the more I learn.
I cannot stop. It's now my turn.
I ask my questions and more return.
Now, my next lesson is to discern.
But now I'm fallen and I'm in the dark.
It's you I'm calling. I need a spark.
Now, what I need is some more heart.
I lay here bleeding. I won't depart.

All I can ask: Who am I?

What is Love?

I thought of her face too often.
I'm often mistaken by my love for my coffin.
I'm coughing from the grip of my conflicts wrapped around my neck,
grip locked in.
I'm losing my life as I tunnel through this tunnel to live life.
To give life, I live right, even when it feels there's nothing I did right.

The day I lost her I never wanted to realize I lost her.
I just wanted to offer my heart to her, I'm fostered.
I've halted my growth to exalt her and show my true love and jolt her.
Now, I look in the mirror when no one is near.
The vision isn't clear because my eyes continue to tear.

Her absence has been given me fear as I try to understand the message
here.
I can't shift the gears because I feel inferior to those living near.

The more I walk, the more I learn.
I cannot stop. It's now my turn.
I ask my questions and more return.
Now, my next lesson is to discern.
But now I'm fallen and I'm in the dark.
It's you I'm calling. I need a spark.
Now, what I need is some more heart.
I lay here bleeding. I won't depart.

All I can ask: What is love?

I got a text from her and I didn't really know what's left to say.
I'm lead astray. Should I talk to her or just ask her to go away?
Should I blame her ways or blame myself for the love decay?
I know my heart was wrecked in ways I never wanted to detect.
I felt the effect as tears rolled down my cheek, I can't forget.....

The way I felt when I would dissect what had us offset and that left a threat.
Now, that we're over, there's a void I just can't fill.
Is this real or am I just over exaggerating the entire deal?
She moved on so fast I wonder, did our love even have a worth?
Was it worth anything to her or am I the only one dealing with this hurt?

The case broke open and I bled so profusely,
I couldn't even hold my life together, except loosely.
We tried to have a truce and love each other truthfully.
I didn't see that it couldn't work without her allowed to abuse me.

Now, I can't stop caring for you no matter how hard I fought.
Now, I wonder what kind of bond that we've got.

The more I walk, the more I learn.
I cannot stop. It's now my turn.
I ask my questions and more return.
Now, my next lesson is to discern.
But now I'm fallen and I'm in the dark.
It's you I'm calling. I need a spark.
Now, what I need is some more heart.
I lay here bleeding. I won't depart.

All I can ask: What is love?

In This Maze

The more I walk, the more I learn.
I cannot stop. It's now my turn.
I ask my questions and more return.
Now, my next lesson is to discern.
But now I'm fallen and I'm in the dark.
It's you I'm calling. I need a spark.
Now, what I need is some more heart.
I lay here bleeding. I won't depart.

All I can ask: why am I trapped in (This Maze)?

I wake up in the morning and I wash my face.
I look myself in the mirror and I can't misplace...
The zombie that I see,
The person that I can't be,
I just want to be free,
But I've lost my place.
I just wanted to live my dream in this life we face.
I guess I'm just not sure what that means because my life's a phase.
I take every step I can and everyday I'm more amazed....
At these days that loses me walking through this maze.

It gets darker the further that I journey through (This maze)
The day's harder, so I pray to God as I hurry through (This maze)
Now I'm wondering why I'm wandering further into (This maze)
I've got questions and comments I'm pondering and murmur into (This maze)

I guess I just lost my direction because I've been completely turned around....
With these bad feelings that I'm detecting,
What's the lesson that I'm learning now?
Is this the path that I'm meant to take?

Is this the feeling of fulfillment?
I truly feel so empty that I could break,
Please take my empty heart and fill it.

Every single morning that I wash my face,
It isn't me looking back through eyes that are over glazed.
I've lost all heart for my actions and my face is seeing grays.
I'm not the person that I'm meant to be,
I've lost myself in this maze.

The more I walk, the more I learn.
I cannot stop. It's now my turn.
I ask my questions and more return.
Now, my next lesson is to discern.
But now I'm fallen and I'm in the dark.
It's you I'm calling. I need a spark.
Now, what I need is some more heart.
I lay here bleeding. I won't depart.

All I can ask: Why am I trapped in (This Maze)?

It gets darker the further that I journey through (This maze)
The day's harder, so I pray to God as I hurry through (This maze)
Now I'm wondering why I'm wandering further into (This maze)
I've got questions and comments I'm pondering and murmur into (This maze)

What does my future hold? Why is their heart so cold?
Why does it seem that I've lost my soul, but I've only lost control?
Why am I taking these steps? What's going to happen next?
Is it due to my wicked heart that my life feels the effects?

The maze seems to be getting more and more narrow.
I can't breathe and my heart is an arrow.
It tried to soar through the sky like a sparrow.
It's stuck in its quiver, so I shiver like Jell-o

Now, I walk in this maze and I'm completely amazed...
Trying to see the sun's light in these days.
In this maze!
In this path I walk it seems I've lost myself.
In this maze!
I've lost all will to talk; I know I'm not myself.
In this maze!
I don't want to be me honestly; honestly I just need some help.
In this maze!

What is My Identity?

It's that all I've ever wanted to be was normal,
But it seems I couldn't fit myself inside the box.
I never fully understood the full idea of being formal,
So, I'm hoping that these rhymes will help me unlock.....
What I'm meant to be and who I'm meant to be,
But it seems I don't fully understand.....
Who I'm supposed to be besides who I want to be,
I guess I don't know who I am.

So, I get to determine my identity, no vermin.
My mind's relearning true love through these sermons.
Now, I can't let go of my past, but I grow from it.
No stomach can stomach what I've stomached without gold nuggets.

Knowledge is increased. I'm unleashed in this feast.
Now, I know what I want and I won't stop until I've reached....
My goals, my soul is whole through this hole that I hold.
I'll unfold though the scroll, gathering what's known from the knoll.

I was buried under varied situations that I've carried.
My cares are extremely scary. There, it's getting hairy,
I couldn't live merry, my heart was a cemetery.
I didn't want to see the varied; I just wanted to be married.

The more I walk, the more I learn.
I cannot stop. It's now my turn.
I ask my questions and more return.
Now, my next lesson is to discern.
But now I'm fallen and I'm in the dark.
It's you I'm calling. I need a spark.
Now, what I need is some more heart.
I lay here bleeding. I won't depart.
All I can ask: What is my identity?

So, I let my mind roam through the zones,
I'm hoping to understand my dome.
My thoughts aren't alone, my heart is a drone.
Now, I'm just thrown, not seeing I'm all alone.

I ask the questions to the air, I don't care about the flare that scares.
I just compare my chair to the orchestra that waits there,
Not aware of the position that I don't share.
I'm not the same as them, I'm different and I will continue in that direction.
I'll have a pure resurrection from this depression, now it's time to make progression.

No longer standing still, feeling bad for the things I never really had.
I'm leaping off of this lily pad, navigating through this water, Iliad.
I'm taking this journey to heart, a new day, a new life, a new start.
I won't depart without playing my part,
Even when it's dark, I'll give my life as a spark.

Now, I battle daily, thoughts in my mind drive me crazy,
But I can't let that phase me from these phases that estrange me
From the God that made me.

The more I walk, the more I learn.
I cannot stop. It's now my turn.
I ask my questions and more return.
Now, my next lesson is to discern.
But now I'm fallen and I'm in the dark.
It's you I'm calling. I need a spark.
Now, what I need is some more heart.
I lay here bleeding. I won't depart.

All I can ask: What is my identity?

Where is My Mind?

The more I walk, the more I learn.
I cannot stop. It's now my turn.
I ask my questions and more return.
Now, my next lesson is to discern.
But now I'm fallen and I'm in the dark.
It's you I'm calling. I need a spark.
Now, what I need is some more heart.
I lay here bleeding. I won't depart.

All I can ask: where is my mind?

There are too many questions, not enough solutions.
My rhymes are stuck in this mind of pollution.
I can't think straight, I live in a cloud of confusion.
I'm losing my inclusion, I constantly live in seclusion.

I stay away from people although I crave their attention,
I fight with depression although it can ne'er be mentioned.
I dream of my demise, wondering if I'll feel deaths extension.
Now, I wonder if life's better than the death of our henchmen.

I can't help but ponder about why my mind just wanders.
There are so many goners and opportunities that I've squandered.
I don't wear armor and now my heart just grows fonder....
Of the love I felt and the help that I've laundered.

Was it all worth it? It's the question that plagued me.
It fazed me. It completely drives me crazy.
My brain saves me. It contains my pain, it shades me.
My questions chase me: Can I chase them down with no answer lately?

The more I walk, the more I learn.
I cannot stop. It's now my turn.

I ask my questions and more return.
Now, my next lesson is to discern.
But now I'm fallen and I'm in the dark.
It's you I'm calling. I need a spark.
Now, what I need is some more heart.
I lay here bleeding. I won't depart.

All I can ask: where is my mind?

There are too many questions, not enough solutions.
My rhymes are designed in a mind of intrusion.
I can't keep my thoughts straight, every thought is loosened.
The self-esteem that I'm losing, it's all from the thoughts that I'm choosing.

I battle with my anger, I get lost in frustration.
I hate when I lose at any battle that I'm facing.
I'm in my room pacing; hoping happiness shows through thought infiltration.
My prayers stop at the ceiling when there's no change I'm embracing.

So, I guess It's time to grow and show where I go when I'm low.
I'm sending prayers to the air till my blessings all show.
I drop to my knees just to see everything that God knows.
I'm on a mission to show the discipline it takes to be pro.

The more I walk, the more I learn.
I cannot stop. It's now my turn.
I ask my questions and more return.
Now, my next lesson is to discern.
But now I'm fallen and I'm in the dark.
It's you I'm calling. I need a spark.
Now, what I need is some more heart.
I lay here bleeding. I won't depart.

All I can ask: where is my mind?

I can't say much, I'm at a loss for words.

When I lost my word everything I face got on my nerves.

I hurt too often, I was breathing while living in a coffin.

I can't sit and speak, I feel like a freak, not sure of the portion I got in.

I got fists of fury that swing in a hurry. I need to stop and think.

I look at the jury while my eyes are blurry. I can't let my love go extinct.

What am I trying to prove? How tough I am? How rough I am?

Does the anger that I have define me as a man?

Am I expressing my property while living in this bodily property?

How does my faith prophet me if my anger shows me as a mockery?

Now, I realize that I need help to control myself while I figure what's next to do.

Everything That I've been dealt I can only blame myself.

What else can I do to make myself new?

Step by step I progress through the process.

I protect myself through the projects, just to build myself with the prospects.

Now, I can't ask questions, I've got to keep stepping,

I know that I'm looking for progression; I can't let myself become lessoned.

The more I walk, the more I learn.

I cannot stop. It's now my turn.

I ask my questions and more return.

Now, my next lesson is to discern.

But now I'm fallen and I'm in the dark.

It's you I'm calling. I need a spark.

Now, what I need is some more heart.

I lay here bleeding. I won't depart.

All I can ask: where is my mind?

Pit and the Pendulum

I was at the bottom of my pit with my mind swinging like a pendulum.
Am I a bad guy playing good or a good guy playing bad?
I guess I'll understand the trends within.
Now, I wait in the darkness, with each thought the blade grows sharper.
My flesh feels each swipe pass; soon the cut will cut so much harder.
I keep thinking to myself,
"Did I do this to myself or am I just the victim?"
Is it because I love pain that I saw my emotion veins and subconsciously
decided to clip them?
Did I see the red flags and ignore them purely due to ignorance,
Or was I being blinded by desire,
Trying to climb higher while figuring out what my image is?
Now, I sit in the pit, the darkness seeps into my consciousness.
My thoughts are lost in this. I can't pray; I lost confidence.
I left love's side and followed the rabbit down the rabbit hole.
I never thought it was radical; it just left me acting like an addict though.
Now, I sit in the pit, the pendulum is precise factor.
Will I let it kill me or will the blades be used to free me?
The questions of my mind after.….

I was at the bottom of the pit with my heart swinging like a pendulum.
Am I meant to be with her or free from her?
I guess I'll never understand the end of them.
I waited for my fate; the rats freed me from my ropes.
Yet, I'm still trapped. Where can I truly go for hope?
Each thought cuts me deep and my heart has taken a beating.
Now, I'm bleeding, but I'm still breathing.
I'm working, I'm not leaving.
I saw the red flags and ignored them instantly.
This caused decent down the pit.
Why didn't I live differently?
Now, I sit in the pit, the darkness seeps into my consciousness.

The conflict is the darkness is trying to kill me, trying to improve my incompetence.

I can't allow that! Even in the darkness there's a light to shine.

Even as I write this rhyme, I fight my mind of shady thoughts,

Ensuring that my light will shine…

So, as the pendulum swings, so does my mindset.

The decision factor is my laughter. True joy has no limit or official time set.

What Can I Say?

I awoke this morning with a single thought on my mind.
I'm happy to be who I am although I still have to find....
I'll find the place that I belong and the person that I'm meant to be.
Now, I see that I am only given what is meant for me.
My heart has been healed, although it took time and patience.
Every day is a new day, now I must look into my life stations.

I thank you God for your heart and your healing hand.
Your patience guides me. Will I finally understand?
I want to be new, so I must be something new.
If I want to see something differently than I've got to change my point of view.
If I wish to walk an alternate path, then I must adjust my foot placement.
If I wish to know you differently, then I must break my security encasement.

So, what can I say? What can I do?
In order to know who I am, I must truly know you.
So, I look into the mirror with your book before me.
Will the puzzle pieces all connect when I'm healed from what tore me?

I woke up this morning with a single thought on my mind.
I'm ready to be who I am. I can't let myself fall behind.
I can rise up, all I have to do is believe and achieve.
There's no time to grieve, with your grace I will stand and succeed.
So, change my point of view for me to keep my eyes on you.
I need to know what's new, but I must follow what's true.

If I don't understand, I pray each step is precise.
Even the backsliding is providing a new appreciation for my life.
I wasn't pulled out of death to be left to die in despair.
I didn't get freed from sin's grip to spend my life lying there.
Help me to comprehend your path and take the step that I need to walk.

I need to spend my time chasing you; you and I need to talk.
So, what can I say? What can I do?
In order to know who I am, I must truly know you.
So, I look into the mirror with your book before me.
Will the puzzle pieces all connect when I'm healed from what tore me?

One Single Step

One single step leads me in the darkness where it left me.
One single wreck left me with hardness as it vexed me.
I turned down a tunnel of torment,
I'm tormented to crumble in a humble fortress.

Now, I won't stay here to spend days here.
I'm a knight at night; I fight to go astray here.

I will hit my knees to send my God my pleas...
To him I'll go! Go! Go!
It's on him I will lean when this life of mine is mean....
I need to know! Know! Know!

One single step leads me to the light where it leaves me.
One single concept that leaves me in the light as it feeds me.
I turned down a path of praise,
I'm praising the son, raising each one, giving us the love of new days.

Now, I will stay here to spend my days here.
I'm a knight in the light as I fight to remain here.

I will hit my knees to tell my God I'm pleased....
To Him I'll go! Go! Go!
It's on Him I lean when this life of mine is mean....
I need to know! Know! Know!

One single step,
Will change everything you've ever seen.
Leave the footprint that is left,
That is not the person you were meant to be.
When the darkness closes in
And there's future that you can see.
It only takes one step to begin,

And the faith that sets us free.

God is my guide, so I will follow.
All else I've seen is dark and hollow.
I'm here today, but gone tomorrow.
Lord, help me find peace, I don't need this sorrow.
I need your love because mine is a desert.
I've been left dry and I can't best serve.

I've lost my heart, I need an intercessor.
Can you make me new? That's the question I must measure.

I will hit my knees to send my God my pleas...
To him I'll go! Go! Go!
It's on him I will lean when this life of mine is mean....

I need to know! Know! Know!
I will hit my knees to tell my God I'm pleased....
To Him I'll go! Go! Go!
It's on Him I lean when this life of mine is mean....
I need to know! Know! Know!

I will take my single step back into my faith.
I will turn away from what I was and embrace what I'll face.
I will take my single step back into my presents.
I will leave the torment for a place that is pleasant.

One single step,
Will change everything you've ever seen.
Leave the footprint that is left,
That is not the person you were meant to be.
When the darkness closes in
And there's future that you can see.
It only takes one step to begin,
And the faith that sets us free.

Oh Thank You, LORD

In my darkest time, when no light was seen,
I was up to fight to outlive my dream.
Yes, I had doubt coursing through my mind.
I had to lift myself when I fell behind.
I had to turn to you to find my joy.
I had to learn to pray when I was annoyed.
I couldn't let myself fall through the cracks.
I will crawl to you because I need you back.

Oh, thank you, LORD.
Oh, thank you, LORD.
Oh, thank you, LORD.
Oh, thank you, LORD.

I never thought I'd walk away from your heart.
I don't know you now and I must restart.
I looked around and saw a cloud above.
Now, I'm alone and I feel no love.
Yet, I'm not stuck because I know you're near.
Let me speak the words that I need to hear.
Let me turn to you because I know you're great.
Let me know your love when the world sees hate.

Oh, thank you, LORD.
Oh, thank you, LORD.
Oh, thank you, LORD.
Oh, thank you, LORD.

I'm standing here waiting to hear your voice.
Your love lifted me up and showed me your choice.
I sought to be healed and you healed me over time.
I needed your grace and you gave me something I'd never find.
Now I'm made new and it's all due to you.

I look into my past and I finally grasp that what you gave is true.
So, thank you LORD for your love and grace,
Thank you for the new life and the new love to chase.

Oh, thank you, LORD.
Oh, thank you, LORD.
Oh, thank you, LORD.
Oh, thank you, LORD.

The Light Pierced the Darkness

The light pierced through the darkness, illuminate my life.
I felt a beat when I thought I was heartless, I even regained my sight.
The light pierces the darkness when I thought it was too thick of a barrier.
Hope was injected into my veins; I guess you can see I'm a carrier.
I've carried before but I left the package in my past.
I found it again and I need it because life without it is a task.
The light pierced my darkness, now I can see clear again.
I see the light; I follow the rays, now I can never end up here again.
A smile on my face, a fresh beat in my heart.
I saw my pain end. I know where His love starts.
He told me that I was fine; He said he had a plan.
The broken pieces of my peace I placed in his hand.
I prayed when I couldn't form sentences, I couldn't even utter.
My love had been given away, never thought I'd love another.
Light pierced the darkness, showing me my healing.
A sensation filled my muscles, now I can keep feeling.

The more I walk, the more I learn.
I cannot stop. It's now my turn.
I ask my questions and more return.
Now, my next lesson is to discern.
But now I'm fallen and I'm in the dark.
It's you that's calling. I see the spark.
Now, what I need is a new start,
I lay here seeing the light pierce the dark.

I feel dry, but I don't feel desolate.
I need to know your love, I can't live life desperate.
I pray you'd feel me up; I need your presence in my heart.
I never want to give up; I pray that you give me a fresh start.
I've been given something new, something great that have orchestrated.

I will follow you through because you've healed me from what left me jaded.
So, I sojourn on and carry on, looking to the light that's pierced,
Through the dark, where it all starts, ensures nothing else interferes.
I'm on a path of love at last; I've finally seemed to take my steps.
The greatest question asked isn't always last; how will I see that I am blessed?
My future is known, neither is it set in stone.
All I know is all along I have never truly been alone.
I see the light, even in the night, although we ignore it in the day.
Now, I see that it's alright because I know you will not lead me astray.
I will walk this path into light from the darkness,
I know that you will guide me through the times that are the hardest.

The more I walk, the more I learn.
I cannot stop. It's now my turn.
I ask my questions and more return.
Now, my next lesson is to discern.
But now I'm fallen and I'm in the dark.
It's you that's calling. I see the spark.
Now, what I need is a new start,
I lay here seeing the light pierce the dark.

Story of Our Future

My ink tells the story of my past,
Your smile tells the story of my future.
My ink reminds me of all I've passed,
All my hidden wounds held together by sutures.
Now, I look into a space so vast,
We're traveling through life of love on a cruiser.
Now, I just look at you and laugh;
I laugh because your love for me is a party booster.

This may be new to us but that doesn't mean it's not worthwhile.
We'll work while we'll live a life of love and work trials.
Let us focus on God and all that He has given us,
He has given us this living love that has driven us.
That's how we know each other and that's how we'll remain.
We can't refrain from his name; it's in that truth that we gain.
I appreciate you. That's all I can say forever more.
Your heart for me makes me love you even more.
I appreciate you and just couldn't wait to tell you.
Your heart for me refreshes my vision on a stale view.

My ink tells the story of my past,
Your smile tells the story of my future.
My Ink reminds me of all I've passed,
All my hidden wounds held together by sutures.
Now, I look into a space so vast,
We're traveling through life of love on a cruiser.
Now, I just look at you and laugh,
I laugh because your love for me is a party booster.

Together we will grow closer to Christ and His great ways.
Our hate stays in the past and we will praise God on our great days.
I will pray for you daily, I will thank God for you nightly.
We will fight the stereotypes of the world to ensure that we live rightly,

I'll have your back through all that we could face,
As we face this race with faith and the love that we embrace.
I appreciate you. That's all I can say forever more.
Your heart for me makes me love you even more.
I appreciate you and just couldn't wait to tell you.
Your heart for me refreshes my vision on a stale view.

My ink tells the story of my past,
Your smile tells the story of my future.
My Ink reminds me of all I've passed,
All my hidden wounds held together by sutures.
Now, I look into a space so vast,
We're traveling through life of love on a cruiser.
Now, I just look at you and laugh,
I laugh because your love for me is a party booster.

We can't deny our connection; all we can do is connect;
Your heart I will protect in this time of love that we select.
So, I ask that guard my heart as I daily place it in your palm.
We will deal with qualms as we pray and remain calm.
I love how great you are; caring, and compassionate.
I love how you're compassionate in times when life's clashes hit.
I appreciate you. That's all I can say forever more.
Your heart for me makes me love you even more.
I appreciate you and just couldn't wait to tell you.
Your heart for me refreshes my vision on a stale view.

My ink tells the story of my past,
Your smile tells the story of my future.
My Ink reminds me of all I've passed,
All my hidden wounds held together by sutures.
Now, I look into a space so vast,
We're traveling through life of love o a cruiser.
Now, I just look at you and laugh,
I laugh because your love for me is a party booster.

Something More Than Myself

I thought I was going crazy; I haven't walked the path yet.
I know I'd take my first step if I didn't realize that my path's set.
I reset my path, yet, I'm not sure I can match it.
My acts set my accent to re-birth life and hatch it.
I dreamed I'd be different throughout my adolescence.
Now, I'm becoming the man I'm not meant to be because I'm reckless.
I want to be seen differently, I guess I've got to add on lenses.
So, I can find my mind; protect this, find my hate, wreck this.

It's time to walk the path and leave the past in the past.
I won't wear it like a mask that has me lost in the past.
I want to shatter expectations that carry in the air waves.
My voice carries expectations that bury cares on my fair days.
I can't live up to what I think. I can't live up to what I say.
Daily my heart will shrink, eventually I'm lead astray.

Now, I have to pray and seek something more than myself.
I'm at war with myself. I need something more than myself.

I thought I had lost it, but I have realized I never really had it.
I've had it. The answers that I've had weren't real, I can't hack it.
I wanted to be different, but I couldn't change my habits.
I tried to transform, but it seems I'm right back at it.
My thoughts are tied up; I guess I can't speak clearly.
The heat is near me, I burn up from the light that beats near me.
I'll smile on even when it's hard to know if He hears me.
I want to quit, but I can't quit; I do what I can to keep cheery.

Yes, I wanted to be different, but I know who I am now.
I will land down on the ground and tell my struggles to stand down.
Now, I know I'm different and it's something I better understand now.
I will use my uniqueness to be a better man now.

It's time to walk the path and leave the past in the past.
I won't wear it like a mask that has me lost in the past.

Now, I have to pray and seek something more than myself.
I'm at war with myself. I need something more than myself.

But what is the Question?

Too often I let my mind wander,
Too often I find myself in an abyss of coherent thought.
I wander through the wondrous catacombs of development.

I'm looking for an answer.
But what is the question......

Too often I let my words form,
Too often I find myself on a journey of entitled language.
I trail through the depths of the deepest consequence.

I've spoken of an answer,
But what is the question.....

What is the question?

It seems that I ask it too often;
Even though the question's it's hidden.
I ask because I know I'm searching:
I'm awaiting the arrival of the everlasting answer.

Just when it seems figured out,
The question keeps changing.
I'm once again I'm left in the darkness to wander,

What is the question?

Down the Rabbit Trail

I've been down the rabbit trail.
In the end all I can tell.
I can't do this by myself,
I need some help. I need help.

I was down in the underground and I was trying to rise out.
I couldn't look down at the ground; I found I had to look to the skies now,
I realized there's the one in the crown, a truth I couldn't deny now.
I had to trust Him. I had to love Him, if I wanted to rise out.

I've been down the trail and well, I must tell that I can't prevail.
I need Christ and His tales, if I ever want my life to not be stale.
I've been down the trail and well, I must tell what I need to tell.
His grace can lift me from this hole. I need Jesus when I fail.

I've been down the rabbit trail.
In the end all I can tell.
I can't do this by myself,
I need some help. I need help.

I was in the pit of despair with no care, trying to see the light.
I was down there trying to breathe air and nothing really seemed right.
So, I sat down there with hatred to share and my future didn't seem bright.
So, while down there I spoke with prayer, hoping I could see right.

Can I pray through this time? Will the prayer reach your ears?
Your grace is something I must find because I no longer can stay here.
The dark thoughts cloud my mind; I need your thoughts to make mine clear.
I see your hope as a sign; I still believe you are near.

I was down in the pit, but that doesn't mean that I'll stay here.

It's time to stand, I can't quit, I've got to kneel down and pray there.
Even when I slip, I tighten my grip and finally find my way there.
It's only through Him that I'm equipped, through the night I see day there.

Now, it's time to rise because I know who my God is.
I know I can be made new because my God is honest.
I know I can make it through, I've just got to pay homage.
In all I do and all I say because I follow who's the strongest.

I've been down the rabbit trail.
In the end all I can tell.
I can't do this by myself,
I need some help. I need help.

The More I Stay

The more I stay down here, the more I face my fears.
I must face my mirror to finally see things clear.
The more I stay down low, the more I learn to know.
It's time to let go so I can finally grow.

I kneel down and pray because I'm thankful for my position.
I realize the steps I took that lead to my deposition.
Now, I'm down in the dumps, given the time to sit and listen.
Now, I must transition to a new level of faith with a decision.

Will I trust in Christ in this life that I am living?
Will I finally see right? Will my heart keep on giving?

Will I choose to love when the world chooses to hate?
Will I find favor in my faith or will it never be that great?
No! I must believe it's great because my God is great.
God knows my fortune and fate; all I can do is continue to wait.

I was placed in this position to listen and to learn.
I needed to trust God in all of life's turns.
This life we live is tough, each hit gets more firm.
Yet, we get tougher the more that we learn.

I kneel down and I pray because I'm grateful for this position.
I realize the steps that I needed to take to get out of this description.
I'm no longer in the dumps, took time to sit and listen.
I'll make the transition with this prayer and description.

Father, I thank you for your wisdom in this time of uncertainty.
You've allowed me to grow in a time that was hurting me.
I've healed and I've grown; through it all, now I know,
I can't forget who I am; I've got to let it show.

The more I stay down here, the more I face my fears.
I must face my mirror to finally see things clear.
The more I stay down low, the more I learn to know.
It's time to let go so I can finally grow.

Printed in the United States
By Bookmasters